Henry Smith Thompson

LETTERS
FROM
SIBERIA

September 1918 to March 1919

Letters home from a senior American Red Cross official
leading relief work in Siberia during the Russian Revolution
at the end of World War I

Edited by Hilary Hullah

Privately published in Oxford, England through Independent Publishing Network

Publication date: 1 May 2021
ISBN 978-1-80049-674-3

Printed in England

Edited by Hilary Hullah

The letters in this book were transcribed by the editor from originals in her possession. Historical and biographical notes, and other commentary, are the original work of the editor.

The pictures of Henry S. Thompson that appear on pages 97*ff* are reproduced from originals in the editor's collection. All other images are taken from publicly available archives and are believed to be in the public domain.

The photos chosen are those which to some extent illustrate a place or scene from the letters. Some are of Omsk whereas others are generic in nature and illustrate aspects of life in Siberia at this time.

Acknowledgements

I owe a great debt to Catherine Andreyev, Emeritus Professor of Russian History at Christ Church, Oxford. Her help has been invaluable in understanding the background to this period of Russian History. She has also supplied me with the newsreel and photographs used in this document. Most of the photographs have been taken from a newsreel of the American military mission in January-February 1919, which can be found in the United States National Archives. Some photographs come from an article written by Maksim M. Stelmak and Dmitry I. Petin of Omsk State Technical University, Historical Archive of the Omsk Region, Russian Federation.

I also owe a great debt to Jonathan Bromley, whose technical skills and creative imagination have helped to make this document come alive. In particular, the arrangement of the pictures and his suggestions with regard to the explanatory information surrounding the letters has made the whole project more stimulating and informative. He has seen the document with new eyes and therefore enabled me to create a more exciting version of these letters. Finally, without his technical expertise I could not have achieved such an accessible account of my grandfather's unique experience.

Hilary Hullah
Oxford, 20th April 2021

Table of Contents

Table of Figures

Preface

I was given these letters by my aunt who said she didn't want them and I could do what I wanted with them. I had no idea what I was going to find. For a while I put off looking at them. Eventually, during the coronavirus lockdown of 2020-2021, I decided I might as well do something with them.

At first, I wondered if they would disintegrate in my hands. As I grew more confident, I started to read them and then type them out, I was struck by the extraordinary experience my grandfather had had at a desperate time in a desperate part of the world. He seemed to be highly motivated to help the refugees he encountered and was pretty determined to stick at a task for which he had had no experience whatsoever. I never met him and was given little information about him by my grandmother or my mother. I knew he came from Ohio, which was beyond the known world as far as my grandmother's family was concerned. I got the impression he was rather quiet and perhaps a bit grumpy. I now have a greater insight into his character and realise that he was a very kind and thoughtful person with a determination to do as much as he could to make the world a better place. He appears to be devoted to my grandmother and his children and has a great appreciation for the natural world as well as a great affection for little children. I also think he was probably a good judge of character and pretty astute about money. At this time, he had not completely found his niche in the world and was wondering what he could do next. This experience must have been life changing for him. I have come to see my grandfather in a completely different light. I am only sorry that I cannot talk with my mother about this as I know she would have been able to shed some light on her father's character.

The letters themselves will have references to some of my grandparents' friends and relatives. They were considering a joint farming project with some dear friends, Mabel and Pinto Cherio. This never came to fruition, but it goes to show that there was some flux in their lives. My grandfather came from a farming family and was proud of the farm which they built and developed on Fairhaven Hill in Concord, Massachusetts. At that time, Concord was a small, closely knit community and my grandparents were well known and active in the town. He was involved in finance and was frequently placed in a position of trust for various financial institutions and charities. As he says in these letters, he felt he wanted to stay in Concord and contribute to the causes he held dear to his heart.

There is much of interest in these letters from an historical point of view. It is a first hand account of this remote part of Russia and the life of the people there. It is also a very distressing picture of the plight of refugees and prisoners of war in the aftermath of the first world war and the beginning of the Russian Revolution. It is shocking to learn of the sufferings we encounter here.

We may think that life is uncertain at the moment as we face the vagaries of a virus, but my grandfather also speaks of the considerable uncertainty of his time. It is quite apparent in the letters that communication was very limited and no one could be sure that a letter would reach its destination. News travelled very slowly and rumours abounded. My grandfather had little real knowledge of how and when the world war would end, nor how far the Russian Revolution was progressing. There was a feeling of chaos as order broke down and violence was very near the surface. These were extremely unsettled times when no one knew what lay ahead and many feared the worst.

I cannot help but admire the courage of my grandfather.

Hilary S. Hullah
April 2021

Jan 8 5:30 P.M.   13.

This has been a very cold day here - The
coldest - it seemed in our cars yet - 40 below
It is a holiday here - The Russians have 3
holidays in succession - Christmas, and
the two following days. This afternoon, as I
did not feel quite up to working, I went
out and distributed about 100 packages of
candy to the people living in box cars
Will you believe it when I tell you
that I did not see hardly one of the 100
children with anything on their feet. Many
of them, when the news spread that I was
coming, ran down the wooden ladders that
lead up to their cars, in their bare feet!
Now just think of it! I went into about 50
Cars, and I do wish I could picture to you
the inside. I can do no better than to let you
imagine how you would get on with your
family living in an American box car - Then
remember the Russian car is only about
½ as long. In the cars there is nothing

14.

but boards put across the cars for beds. People lie on these often without anything under them. Coal, wood, all their living utensils, stove, are there of course; and the floors are dirty and cold. Such conditions you can't even imagine; you have to see them. My how happy the small ones were to get the little red and blue packages of candy; and most of them thanked me and bowed down almost to the floor. I am living in a world the like of which I never dreamed existed. — The Canadian soldiers have begun to arrive here. Today I saw many of them well groomed and fitted out for artic work. We hear to-night that the Japs are to come over

This example of the original letters is transcribed on page 71. It describes the appalling living conditions of some of the refugees, and the story of how Henry Thompson delivered Christmas gifts to as many children as he could.

Background information on the Russian Revolution

The Russians remained united throughout World War I, but suffered huge losses of life and experienced severe food shortages. The people resented the part played by Tsar Nicholas II and riots followed. There was a general strike in February, 1917. In March, the Tsar was forced to abdicate and a weak provisional government took charge. At the same time, a council called the Petrograd Soviet of Workers' and Soldiers' Deputies was working towards change and gained popularity. At this time, Lenin who led the Bolshevik faction of the Russian Soviet Democratic Party, was exiled in Zurich for Marxist activities. The Germans helped him return to Russia, but the leader of the Provisional Government, Alexander Kerensky, ordered his arrest and banned the Bolsheviks. Lenin then fled to Finland. In August 1917, the Bolsheviks gained control of the Petrograd Soviet and Lenin was able to return to Russian confident that the Bolsheviks would be able to seize power.

Lenin decided to act quickly. When the Red Guard took control of Petrograd on the 26th of October, 1917, the Provisional Government surrendered. The Bolsheviks were now in control. Lenin shut down the Russian Constituent Assembly in January of 1918 and created a Marxist one-party state.

Lenin and his new Bolshevik government then proceeded to sign an armistice with the Central Powers in December 1917. This led to the Treaty of Brest-Litovsk in March 1918 whereby Russia lost control of the Baltic States and the Ukraine and paid 6 billion German marks in reparations. Many Russians were angry that they had lost so much and opposed the Bolsheviks, who were a minority in Russia.

Lenin then proceeded to launch a campaign of "Red Terror" against anyone who was thought to be a threat to this regime. The new Bolshevik secret police, the Cheka, used intimidation to achieve their ends. Subsequently, civil war broke out between the Bolsheviks, the "Reds" and the anti-Bolshevik forces, which were composed of the White Army, formed of Tsarist supporters and military officers. Britain, France and the United States also supported the Whites as they feared the spread of communism. The Allied forces offered support to Admiral Kolchak, who led the White Army whose government was based in Omsk.

Despite this international support, the Bolsheviks had better organisation and the brilliant leadership of Leon Trotsky. Furthermore, they controlled Moscow and Petrograd, which were industrialised cities and encompassed Russia's railway network. After four years of bitter warfare, the Bolsheviks gained control of Russia in October 1922.

The letters

Hotel St. Francis, Union Square, San Francisco
September 9. 1918

My dear,

We arrived here this p.m. in good shape. By the time you get this note I shall be far out on the briny if the plans work out.

We shall have some interesting comparisons to make in the shape of war correspondents, etc. I have already made the acquaintance of two: one particularly interesting because he is a Russian and wants much to teach me the language. He will be a great help to me. I am reading Russian books madly. One I am returning to you to read. I'll send others back from Honolulu. Went to see "Jack O Lantern" in Chicago with Stone of Montgomery and Stone fame. Very much of an extravaganza - good time killer and diverter of thought. Also went to see the War Exhibit which was really remarkable. Many relics from the battle field and a sham battle over hundreds of acres with trenches, wire entanglements, courier pigeons, tanks and such a noise when 1000's of guns, cannons, mortar, stars, etc. went off. You never heard such a din in your life. The Yanks, largely Marines, went over the top and, of course, took 100's of Germans. You never saw such a mix up in your life. Red Cross men carrying off the wounded, soldiers bringing in prisoners, real thing you know. Thousands of spectators yelling, babies crying, women crying, etc. I wish you could have seen it. Well, my dear, I should never feel like leaving all you dear ones at home for so long if I could be satisfied not to do what little I can to help out in this great struggle. I feel <u>terribly</u> at not being able to do something more active. I envy the lowest private. But everybody, officers and all, were so nice to us at the War Exhibit. They would not let us pay to go in and the Commanding Officer had us at his headquarters after the show. They all seem to think we are the real thing (I mean the Red Cross).

It makes me feel so stupid to wear a uniform. I find so many people, particularly in the West, who do not know what we are! Call us English Aviators, Colonels, etc! I don't wonder they are confused. There are so many, many different kinds of services all with different uniforms travelling about.

I have written Adeline and George Whiteside, Mabel and Pinto, Mrs. Blandy, Aunt Annie, etc. My dear I am trying not to worry but I must confess you are on my mind <u>as much</u> now as the children. Do be careful. <u>Don't worry about me or money matters.</u> It wouldn't be fair to do so now under the circumstances. We will all be together again soon and will be happy and able to enjoy the children.

There are so many things I want to do with you later on. Won't it be fun to go off with Mabel and Pinto? Also to visit "Tuilleyers" again! I expect to keep a diary on this trip and I wish you would keep the letters I write you from Siberia, etc. for they may have something that will help me if I ever should want to write up my experiences.

You will hear again from me soon as I shall drop you another note before I sail. Do be careful of yourself and the dear chicks. Kiss them all for me <u>now.</u>

Love, Henry

San Francisco, September 12 1918

My dear,

Your telegram packed full of news came a little while ago. I can't tell you how it cheered me. I next expect to hear from you all the through the American Red Cross at Honolulu, where I expect to arrive about September 21. You had better have into the hands of Mr. Otis H. Cutler by the 20th any message. Be sure to have a message saying "all well" if nothing more. Also, same into Mr. Cutler's hands <u>by Oct. 2</u> a message for me when I reach Yokohama on the 3rd. Mr. Cutler's address is simply ARC Washington. Beyond Yokohama you can always reach me through ARC Washington and they will also forward you messages from me.

I hope to have some photographs for you both in ARC and US uniforms.

Glad to know everything goes on so well at home. <u>Do not worry about anything</u> and I will try not to.

Give love and kisses to all and keep heaps for your dear self.

Ooooo Henry

San Francisco (Hotel St. Francis)
September 14, 1918

My dear,

I am not sure (nobody is) that the boat will go today. So many people, crew and others, are within the draft age, and there is endless confusion. I am expecting, however, that this is the last letter you will get until the one I mail from Honolulu reaches you. I am sending an express package in which are two books on Russia which I hope you will have time to read. Please save my letters from this date on unless they are entirely personal. I have had some Kodaks snapped of myself in RC uniform which if they develop will be forwarded to you. I hope to get you some others from Japan.

Do you know the only thing we left out was the dressing gown? I'll have to get one in Japan, though I should like one on the boat.

I am so glad Rob has got back. It really means so much to all of you. The only thing now is to take care of yourselves and be happy.

Love and kisses to all.

Ooooo H.

San Francisco (Hotel St. Francis)
September 14, 1918

Dear Helen,

We do sail today.

The books I spoke of sending will go by Parcel Post instead of Express.

Beautiful day – good war news – good health and spirits – all I lack is an intimate goodbye with all of you.

Love and kisses, Ooooo H

Enroute S.F. to Honolulu, September 17, 1918

3.30 p.m.

Dear Helen,

We have now been out just three days. The weather has been cloudy most of the time but it is bright today. The sea has been somewhat rolly but not so bad as to affect many people. It is much warmer than when we started. I have worn my light weight RC uniform and have been comfortable. I am quite all right in every respect except that the indigestion which I developed in Washington has not yet cleared up. I am careful about eating. There is no very good opportunity for exercise.

There are about 800 passengers aboard (3 classes) Among these are approximately [censored] [1]

Among the notables are C. R. Crane (of the Root Commission to Russia), Dr. Paul Reinsch, our new Minister to China, Herman Bernstein, Correspondent of the New York Herald on his way to Siberia to be attached to the same Army as we. There are missionaries with their families (many children) on their way to China and many young school teachers (women) on their way to the Phillipines. There are many orientals; women and men, on their way home. The ship is new and comfortable, food good – all Chinese help. Waiters dressed in long, white mother hubbard gowns (blue for lunch and dinner) with white stockings and slippers – all so clean and neat, short hair, no gloves. The trip is so long, 18 days to Yokohama, 31 to Manilla, that a long series of entertainments has been arranged. Athletic and deck sports, singing and dancing, etc. I am Chairman of the Finance Committee. All money goes to the Red Cross, etc. I am doing a great amount of reading, mainly on the countries I expect to visit.

---

[1] *These letters were censored, probably by the White Russian government. Each censored item has been marked in the text.*

Sept. 20

We are now one day out of Honolulu. Expect to arrive there tomorrow evening and leave next morning. I am sorry we are to have so short a stay there as I do not know when I shall see the place again. I <u>hope</u> to come home via Europe. If I do not, I shall plan to stop off at Honolulu on the way back.

From the scrappy wireless news we get daily, I am inclined to think that the Central Powers are going to have a pretty restless winter. We shall hear a great deal about peace, but I think they will hardly make any proposals that the Allies can consider. Therefore, I believe the end is some distance off yet.

Please see that our trees are looked after this fall. The apple trees should have old wire removed and larger wire put on. They seemed to me very thick and bushy and need a good deal of pruning. I should also prune other fruit trees and be sure to put out new trees where old are missing in hen yard. Also grapes in the row killed by lightning. Also trim spruce hedge.

I suppose by this time you are having grapes. I saw some enormous clusters in California. I am afraid we shall not have much fruit to eat in Siberia though a woman on board tells me she never had better food than she got in Vladivostok last Spring. There are so many small children aboard. One next door only six months old, howls a great deal.

September 20, 1918   Enroute to Honolulu

Dear Chicks,

There are many children on board and I play games with them every day. There are two little girls whose mother is an Austrian and father a Chinese and they are the most interesting actors I have ever seen. They are so so sturdy and can do anything that takes strength. They are not so good at games that take brains. They do not play checkers or dominoes anything like so well as you do, and yet they are almost as old. They won the potato race yesterday. They are very queer looking.

I am thinking of you both as going to school every day. I hope you are as fond of going as you were when I saw you there last winter. I wonder whether you would enjoy travelling on a large ship? It gets rather tiresome especially on so long a trip as this. Just think of it, 18 days penned up on a boat! What do you think you would do to pass the time? Well, I'll send you some picture postals from Honolulu and then from Japan. I wish you look on the map and see where I am going. It will be frightfully cold in Siberia, people tell me. I am going to buy some fur lined boots and a sheep skin overcoat. It is a great country for furs.

Well, good bye and lots of love to all,

Father

The names of the Austro-Chinese girls are Mina and Poldi Long. Aren't they pretty names?

Sept. 21 2 p.m.

We can just see land. Due to dock about 6 p.m.

We had a big show on board last night. It is surprising how much talent there is on board a ship. There were all kinds of amateur acting. The best I thought was a Chinese trick artist. I never saw such stunts, swallowing a bunch of needles, taking a chicken out of a handkerchief, etc. Raised about $55 which will be used in buying tobacco for the sailors, etc. who are aboard. We expect to entertain them on shore tonight.

September 21, 4:30 p.m.

Just pulling into quarantine.

More from shore.

Love and kisses to all.

Ooooo Henry

Half way between Honolulu and Yokohama
September 27, 1918

10 a.m.

My dear,

There are many messages I want to send you that it is discouraging to begin writing them. In the first place, I was more than disappointed not to get any word from you at Honolulu. I think it <u>must</u> be the fault of the RC at Washington. I left word at Honolulu if your message came late to have it forwarded by wireless to the boat, but up to date no word and I have given up hope. However I am going on the theory that no news is good news for I know I should hear if everything were not alright.

I had altogether too short a stay at Honolulu. I did not get to see the surf boating except from the ship at a distance. But I saw all that was possible to see in a short time. I did not see Mabel's brother but talked with him over the telephone. He was <u>extremely</u> nice and I am so sorry I could not see him. Of course he was surprised beyond words to hear from Mabel in such a way.

While I think of it, the mails are so uncertain that I want to speak <u>now</u> of Christmas. Please get the children and others something for me. Kellogg will give you the money. I am going to try to send some small trinkets from Japan, but I do not know that they will reach you in time, or ever. I think there is a chance that I may be in the Phillipines for Christmas, but it is <u>very</u> uncertain and I cannot possibly tell this far ahead.

A boat is such a small place and people find so little to do that they waste most of this time getting up rumors (some bad ones), gossip and form cliques. I do wish you could hear the stories that go around this boat every day – some even involving the honor of the most distinguished passengers. I take very little stock in them – my <u>sole</u> vice aboard being poker playing.

Nearly everybody who looks at the pictures of the children takes "Bruzz" for a girl! I suppose that is a compliment. He must be handsome if you can believe people. I know you would not like my looks now for I have just come back from the barber and he gave me a military hair cut for sure. I am reading a very interesting book on the life of the early missionaries (mostly from N.E.) in Hawaii, and also a book on Japan by Clarke. Mr. C. R. Crane (who by the way is related to Wilfred Wheeler) loaned me the former.

Tonight A.L.Castle and I spoke at a meeting of the passengers. He spoke on Hawaii and I on the Red Cross. We had some good singing and the meeting went off very well. I certainly have to pay the penalty of wearing a Red Cross uniform. Somebody is constantly after you to do this or that or to find why the RC doesn't do this or that. After we get to Siberia we expect to go down through China, Japan, Korea, Phillipines, etc. visiting the chapters, urging them to make supplies suitable for Siberian relief. I know we shall have a great time. I hear there are endless squabbles and factions among these foreign chapters.

Of all the children on the ship there is one in particular that I am interested in. It is not a particularly well born child and is rather queer looking – bow-legged – almost negro features – but you never saw such a good natured creature - always smiling and so good. Its parents, especially the father, have very little sense. He feeds the little thing on chewing gum, etc. What do you think of that? It can't be over 2 ½ years old. These missionaries seem to have a good many children and on the whole they are not a very prepossessing lot – not much improvement on their parents. I never could see why God had to make them so homely if they are his chosen ones! Poor things, I am sorry for them they lead <u>such</u> narrow lives.

The Nanking Souvenir - September 30, 1918

Speech given by Henry S. Thompson on the S.S.
Nanking going out to Vladivostok

Red Cross in Siberia

A statement of the plans of the American Red Cross for aid to Siberia will doubtless interest the passengers. Red Cross is already active in the field there doing work mainly among the civilian population under the direction of Dr. R. B. Teusler of Tokyo. But the enormity of the task and the fact that the U.S. now has troops there make the demand for more men and supplies very urgent. Messrs. Castle and Steward and I are going there to assist in organising for bigger work. There are now on the way to Vladivostok about fifty freight car loads of shoes, blankets, shirts, sweaters, socks, cloth, field kitchens, trucks, hospital supplies,

Fig. 1: Dr Teusler (left)

tents, etc. which constitute the advance shipment of supplies.

The work to be done there may be divided roughly into three classes: aiding the civilian population and refugees, which is the greatest, furnishing hospitals, clothing, etc. for the Czech-Slovak army, and thirdly, looking after our own troops in the way of furnishing them with convalescent houses, canteen service and comforts generally, such as they have in France.

After the work has been organized there, Mr. Castle and I will visit the chapters of the American Red Cross throughout the Orient urging and directing them to put their efforts into making supplies available for the needs of Siberia.

Fig. 2: American Red Cross packages from Vladivostok

October 2, 1918

11:30 a.m.

We have just begun to see small fishing fleets out from Japan - queer little boats. They seem to have a large boat along with them. Probably the mother boat with supplies, etc. We can also just see land through the very misty, cold rain that has been falling all morning. I saw yesterday morning a whale that spouted water many times and seemed to be playing else I cannot understand why they came to the top so frequently.

12:30 a.m.

Well I have had enough of water travelling for a while – but there is still some more between us and Siberia – we expect to cross the Japan Sea. We can see the mainland now very clearly.

It seems from here to be very much wooded. (I am sorry to tell you that I have had a fierce time with indigestion on this trip. I have tried to be careful in eating and have done no drinking – a little smoking – but I have been entirely unable to shake it. I must get rid of it before going into Siberia where I hear the food is not any too good. I am thoroughly awake to the seriousness of it and will take the best of care.) We expect to stop at the Grand Hotel in Yokohama and I certainly hope we shall have some word from you there. When we shall go on to Siberia I cannot tell till I get to Yokohama. I certainly have thought <u>volumes</u> about you on this trip. I was so much relieved to hear you were alright when I left San Francisco. I cannot tell when I shall see you again – but I fully realize that there will already be great changes. I have never thought more about the subject than on this trip. I suppose it is because I have fewer things to occupy my mind. Do be careful and above all things happy. Give my love and kisses to the chicks and keep more than I can tell you for yourself. I am going to close this letter now so as to be able to mail it at once on shore. I will drop you a card telling you we are on shore.

Much love, Ooooo Henry

The Grand Hotel Yokohama
Saturday, Oct. 5th, 1918

My dear,

After a very full day yesterday I returned to my room in the hotel about 11 a.m. and found the cable from you. I can't tell you how much it means to hear from you all when I am so far away. Nothing in the world gives so much relief. There are troubles galore here and ahead of us in our work but they can be overcome if I am sure everything at home is right.

Yesterday we were busy all day at the Japanese Red Cross headquarters. They are older at the job than we and we got several valuable suggestions especially with reference to cold weather clothing. I wish you could have seen me dressed up in one of their Siberian uniforms. I stood beside Baron Ishiguro, the President, and was photographed. I may be able to show you the picture some day.

We lunched with the Baron who cannot speak English. It was quite a function and I had to reply with a short speech in answer to his felicitous address of welcome. You can't imagine how here in the Orient everything in the way of form counts for much. We are treated as though we are the representatives of a foreign power and the formalities of bowing and courtesy are never-ending.

In the evening after dining at an American home, we went to the 4th Liberty-Loan drive where Mr. Castle and I were called upon to speak. It is all so strange.

It would be useless for me to try to give you a picture of my impressions of Japan. The constant click of wooden shoes on the street – the babies tied on their mothers' or nurses' backs – the smell of fish, fish sticks, etc., the rickshaws are the things that you first notice. I have not seen much of the rural life yet, but we are going today – Sunday- for a long automobile trip. The weather here is very gloomy, raining most of the time, a little raw and cold. I never saw people packed closer together in living quarters, not even in the tropics. The streets are narrow, the houses on one street backing up against those on the next, and the tiniest little houses about as big for a family of six as the living room in Mamie's house. It looks very funny to see them squatted on the floor.

7:30 p.m. October 6

We have just returned from an automobile trip through the country. I can't for the life of me see how your brother could have been so infatuated with it, but I can't now go into details.

You can write me c/o American Red Cross, Vladivostock, Siberia and it may reach me. I expect to be there until December 1st at least and maybe longer. And if I go away then I shall probably return there.

October 7, 6:30 a.m.

It is still raining. We have a busy day ahead of us before sailing tonight for Siberia. We will be due there Thursday morning.

I do hope you are alright. I think I am some better this morning though I have had a fierce time with my insides. I'll let you hear as often as there is opportunity – and you can always reach me via RC Washington. Give lots of love and kisses to the chicks and look after them until I get back. I know you will. And be particularly careful of yourself. Don't worry. Au revoir.

Ooooo Henry

1st letter from Siberia, October 15, 1918

Dear Helen,

Roger Merriman has just got his orders to go to France via America, and I am hurrying this note through so as to send it off by him. I am dining with him tonight for the last time. I can't tell you how I shall miss him, as I know him better and he is more congenial than any of the few Americans I know over here. It makes me homesick somewhat, but of course I cannot think of leaving yet. Indeed there is so much work here of a kind that is absolutely urgent that I fear I shall be here all winter. The work is with refugees who are constantly pouring into this town from the West. Their condition is so pitiable that one cannot see them and not feel like doing everything possible. I am going to give the whole of my time to this work although I came out to do military relief and have had no experience in this. Most of the poor things are women and children and they have travelled for miles, literally 1000's of miles in freight cars with just enough food to keep them alive and hardly any clothing. It almost kills me to see the little tots. I saw yesterday 135 women and children (Russian Jews) living in a cellar, and such conditions you cannot even imagine. I am tearing up Heaven and Earth to get them into some huge masonry barracks of which, fortunately, Siberia is full. These buildings are of the most substantial character and are not being used by Russian soldiers now. There are 100s of them throughout Eastern Siberia and they certainly are a godsend at this time when there is such need of them. Cold, of course, is the great thing to fight against here and these buildings are built with 3 foot walls, well heated and lighted, so that all who can get in will be warm at least. But there will be thousands throughout central and western Siberia whom we shall not be able to shelter or feed because of the lack of facilities. Fortunately, great quantities of Red Cross warm materials (shoes, sweaters, blankets, etc.) are arriving and we are planning to distribute them as fast and equitably as possible. I hope to be able to keep some kind of a readable account of the work here so as to give you an idea of the country, people, etc. But you know how difficult it is to get any time to write.

We are living in a large room in a private house and boarding at the R.C. canteen where about 40-50 R.C. workers, largely women nurses, board also. Food is good here and at the "Golden Horn", the best restaurant here, the food is perfectly delicious. I never ate better. The streets are packed with the most motley crowds you can imagine – largely soldiers, etc., of every nationality under the sun. I hardly ever hear a word spoken that I can understand. I <u>do</u> wish I could understand for it is an awful handicap to getting along not to understand the language. I don't believe I shall ever be able to acquire it. It unquestionably is hard and I am no longer young!

Sunday, Roger, Al Castle and I took a long drive into the country, dismissed the automobile, had lunch, and then walked for miles along the shore of the ocean. It reminds me of the coast of Maine in many ways – high rugged cliffs and rocky shores. It was a most beautiful day – just like a warm October day at home – and I did enjoy the outing so much. I am looking forward very much to the winter here when I think it will be very interesting driving out to feed the refugees in the barracks situated far out among the hills. We shall need warm clothing. - I hope to be able to get you, dear, some furs, but it's too early to buy them cheap now. There are some very pretty ones <u>perfectly white</u>, not ermine but a kind of rabbit.

You will be glad to learn that my stomach is acting very much better. I was really quite worried for a while. I have almost stopped smoking, am chewing madly and taking care of myself the best I know how. I <u>do</u> miss you so and would give anything to be with you and the chicks tonight. I think <u>all the time</u> of you and could not be reconciled to your party next spring if I did not feel that you are entirely happy about it. It may be that I shall not even be present; you know that I am so far away and I shall probably never get another chance of seeing the Orient again. I wish I knew the <u>approximate</u> date. What a lovely time I am missing by being away from you <u>at this time</u>! Never such a chance again! There's one thing about being away from you for so long a time: I feel almost like being married anew to you when I return

We are very much excited here tonight on war news. We hear that Germany has acceded to all Wilson's terms and has begun withdrawing troops from all enemy countries. I can't believe it to be true. In my case it will not make any difference in my work for this winter. The suffering will go on just the same war or no war for this winter at least.

Well, this note is to be taken to the States by Roger and mailed there so you will be sure to get it. He also says he will call you up when he comes to Cambridge. I know you will be glad to hear direct.

Now as for Christmas, I do wish I could do something, but you understand the difficulties. Be sure to give the children something for me. Now dear, I would give anything to <u>see</u> you tonight – and am consoled only by the feeling that you are all well and happy. Write me c/o Red Cross (I hope you have already) and tell me all the news and I will write often. Much love to all and many kisses.

Ooooo Henry   11 p.m. 10/15/18

Vladivostok, October 23, 1918

My dear,

Well we are at last off (tomorrow) for the front. There have been delay after delay. There will be 30 of us (men and women) on the train and we shall live in it for six weeks. Also a military escort of 6 Americans, 6 Czechoslovaks. We had to make a dining car out of the freight car – impossible to get a regular diner. The compartments in which we live are very comfortable – two persons in each. I have with me a Mr. Yarrow who once lived in Auburndale. We shall, of course, make many stops and establish refugee camps. The work is fascinating in a way, but never again for me. I simply can't stand seeing children hungry and cold. I do not look forward with any pleasure to this winter. By the time you get this letter, I shall be in the thick of it. I have plenty of warm clothing – shall soon have heavy furs. I wish I were in a little better shape physically. I have really been quite miserable with indigestion. I am using every precaution with my health and hope to be alright again soon.

I find myself wondering a good deal these days, in spite of all I have done, what I am going to do when it is all over in about a year. It looks to me now as though I should be free in about a year. I should, of course, like something that would keep me near Concord (I mean near Boston) but this may not be possible. I see a great many difficulties in the way of the farm project with Mabel and Pinto. I should like to keep our permanent home in Concord and I shall do so if it is humanly possible. I have just begun to realize that I am getting old. I really never have before. I should like to work hard about ten years more then give my time to some civic or charitable thing.

I plan now to come home via Europe if possible. I shall be in Western Siberia next spring I think and it will be about as quick as back <u>via</u> Pacific. Besides I want to see the great battle fields, Norway, Sweden, Italy, Egypt, etc. if I can. But it is too soon to make any plans in the present.

I hear Langdon Warner is working for the RC west of here about 3,000 miles. Mrs. W is not with him. People who know him say he is as casual as ever.

I do wish I had asked you to write me at <u>V</u>. I did not think I was to be here long, but it makes me homesick to see everyone else getting letters. I have had but one message from you since I left the U.S. and that was over two weeks ago. I should like to know all the news, where is Rob stationed? What is he going to do when he is discharged?

We get very little war news here, but there is a feeling now that the war will be over this winter. <u>I do hope and pray</u> that the Allies will not allow those hell-hounds to beg off. Unconditional surrender and nothing else.

Well, much love and kisses to you and the dear chicks. They are just getting up now. It is 10 p.m. here.

Ooooo H

Omsk, Siberia, November 8, 1918

Dear Ones all,

I am writing this letter or starting to write from my cabin in the Red Cross Train sitting near the station at Tomsk. This is the most cultured and refined city of Siberia. It is older than America's first settlements, having been founded in 1604. It is a typical Russian city, I am told. The only university in Siberia is located here. I have driven all morning in one of the small Russian sleighs looking for a building in which to establish a hospital. It has been most interesting because we looked at girls' schools, commercial schools, colleges, etc. They were all in session and we had a good chance to see how they run their institutions over here. (The train has started to go, so my writing will be shaky.) It is difficult for me to give you a picture of the school children, the teachers, the class rooms, kitchens (some were boarding schools), laboratories, etc. They were splendid, and in some respects quite up to ours. The little boys and girls were quite well dressed, especially as to outer garments. They wore big fur coats – belted at the waist, with fur caps covering their ears and mostly felt boots, though some wore high leather boots as we used to wear as children. Their faces were bright red and they seemed the picture of health. And there were some poor; I saw many with nothing on their bare legs – only a poor covering for their feet and a thin shawl for their head. In the kitchens were great brick stoves with kettles of soup, cabbage, potatoes, and oh such huge loaves of black, sour, rye-bread which they seem to thrive on. And always tea; in fact you see more tea and black bread than all other foods put together in Russia.

Sugar is here about $1.50 to $2.00 a pound! Think of it! You can imagine how much the poor can use at those prices. In some parts of the country there is much honey. They make delicious candy and pastry here in normal times. I have bought some, but it is <u>very</u> dear now. Not everybody has a well and people generally get their water from big wells in the street. They carry it in buckets fastened at the ends of poles which they balance over their shoulders, a bucket on each end.

The poor dressed, look very much like bundles of rags twaddling along. I think they put on their clothes in the beginning of winter and do not take them off till Spring. To see them at the stations sleeping on the floors, waiting, sometimes days, for trains, all huddled together is a sight which you have to get used to to stand. They make their tea from hot water which they can get at every station. This they drink, children and all, with their black bread. Everything one needs to live on is so abnormally high in this neighbourhood as to be simply out of the question. There are no clothes (cloth), shoes, oil, sugar, or any of the ordinary necessities. We paid today $1.20 a pound for honey. Sugar is $2.50 at the station we are now leaving. Thank heavens there is plenty of cabbage, milk, cheese, butter and rye bread though the latter is 150 times its normal price. The suffering consequent on such conditions will be terrible before this long winter is over. Winter is here now: there is snow and the thermometer is about - +10 to 0. Winter does not break up till May.

As you know, I came to Russia to do work with our own soldiers, but the need for help in caring for the refugees was so great that I could not resist the appeal. I don't know anything of such works. I have never had any experience in social or philanthropic work; but the need is so desperate that I am going ahead because there is no one else to do it. You know, of course, that all mail is censored and therefore you must not expect to hear all from me by letter. I have had experiences to date that would harrow you beyond belief. It is simply a nightmare and if I live through it all, I'll tell you sometime. My own health, unfortunately, is not what it should be and it is not helped by this work.

4:30 a.m. November 9

We have just stopped at Nova Nickoliovitch. It is still so dark that I cannot tell what the day will be like. It is not very cold.

I understand there are 4000 children here refugees from European Russia, who are without anything. I am going to see as soon as it is light. We are so far away from our base of supplies, (and there are no supplies at the base!) 6000 versts, 4000 miles, that it is next to impossible to get things moved out here. We started from Vladivostok on October 24th, and here we are on November 9th. The engines are so poor and there are so many delays that it seems hopeless. I feel about as you would feel going out to feed 150 starved chickens with a teaspoonful of grain. It's not money but supplies we need. There has been quite hard fighting here within the last week – about 200 were killed on November 1 in the town we left yesterday. There is evidence of war everywhere and one thing that delays us so much is military trains. We are treated finely by the R.R.Co and are hurried by as fast as they possibly can. If you glance at the map you will see we are approaching Omsk where I fully expect to spend the winter as I believe it will be as near to the centre of the refugee work as we can get so long as the fighting front remains where it now is, i.e. just west of the Urals. I expect to take a journey over to the front and then come back probably to Omsk as headquarters from which to direct the work. The Czechs, who are the only ones doing much fighting, are a fine people. I have seen a great deal of them since I came out to Siberia and I think they are alright. We have some as waiters and general helpers on this train, and they are splendid fellows. They are all so polite; never failing to salute as sometimes our own boys do. The Italians, I think, make on the whole the most showy, spick-and-span outfit. They look so fine with their green uniforms and the Chausseurs with red feathers in their green hats. The French look so well kempt and the English officers are superb, but the men look a little heavy mentally. There are thousands of prisoners of war here. I spent a great deal of time at stations talking to the Germans and Austrians. I can get on quite well with them and they are so interested to hear anything. Poor creatures, most of them were captured very early in the war and have been up here in Siberia for over four years. Most or many of them have families at home and they are so anxious to hear from them. I find they have had no news. I have been telling them that Bulgaria and Turkey and possibly Austria had given up. It is hard to make some of them believe it. They say Germany can never be whipped! Poor things – the rude shock they are in for. Generally speaking, they are nice fellows. Big open faces, blue eyes, light hair and not mean looking or vicious. Some of their officers are touchy – I wanted to photograph a group and an officer made all the Germans get out of the group leaving only the Austrians, Turks, etc. - neither would he allow the Germans to accept some cigarettes which we tendered. All most of these poor fellows are interested in is to get home. They constantly ask me, "Well why, if the war is over, can't we go back home?" I imagine some of them will and would help raise the devil with the group that got them into this mess if they could only get back home.

Many thousands of them they tell me have starved or frozen to death in the cars along the tracks in past winters.

I have just visited the refugees here. If such conditions existed in the suburbs of any American city, the people thereof would not sleep until they were relieved. Crowded into cars, barracks, so closely that the air knocks one down when you open the doors, are men, women, children, little children with not sufficient clothing to go out into the cold, day after day they spend in these hovels. And the sick, too. I saw 25 convalescents from typhus crowded into double-decked, dark barracks so that their pale faces looked like ghosts as you opened the door and looked in on their

Fig. 3: Soldiers with refugees

stenchy quarters. How they live over night, no one knows. And alas! Many do not; but I must not try to tell you more of this misery until I see you.

Russia, with all its grand expanses of rich plains; its beautiful trees, and the soft-dry snow covering the great fir trees, should be a charming place to live. You hear constantly the jingle of sleigh bells. You imagine the inside of warm houses, you see children coasting (I see two boys now) and skating, piles of fire wood, grey fur coats and you think if only there were no dark side what a place to enjoy life! The people seem so kind and big, and simple like overgrown children. I think they have very little knowledge of organizations; and there is a rough brutality to their natures that causes them to overlook or at least not think of the suffering of others. They seem to pass it by as the most commonplace of things and show the greatest curiosity when you inquire into anything that looks to you as though it needed help.

I haven't had much opportunity to see how they live in their homes. Their tables, their living rooms, beds, etc. are yet unknown to me for I have been living on our train or at R.C. Canteen since I came to Russia; but I mean soon to find out. I want to see how the well-to-do as well as the poor live. I have had in Vladivostok some very good cooking, especially Mongolian pheasants which they prepare most deliciously; also beef-steak and pastries. Cabbage soup is also a great dish with the poor and it certainly is good. I ate what we would call sour 'clobber' which they serve in glasses in the restaurants. It is very good for the stomach! (This will give you some idea of what is bothering me.) Their black rye-bread is sour; and said to be very good for the stomach. They are the greatest bread-eaters I ever saw. It is said they often eat 2 pounds at a meal. You can see them carrying in their arms the hugest loaves – really as big as a ½ bushel basket. Poor people, they have to cut down on bread now.

Sunday morning, November 10, 1918

Warm wind blowing from North, seems as though it might bring rain; I have seen many such days in Ohio, N.E. and in the States generally.

4:30 p.m. arrived at Omsk (see map) a city normally of 100,000, now 500,000 increase due to refugees. This will give you some idea of the size of the problem. I hope none of you will ever be permitted to see such sights. People sleeping in every conceivable place. Every broken shed, box or anything that will make a covering. This city is the centre or capital of the government (what little government there may be!). We hear all kinds of war news tonight but of course are wholly unable to tell how much of it is true. We hear that Turkey and Austria have both surrendered. The Emperor of Austria has abdicated; even the Kaiser has abdicated; that the peace delegates have begun to assemble in Paris, that peace will be declared by Christmas, etc., etc. Yet, within a short distance west of us they are still fighting (the Czechs <u>vs</u> the Bolsheviks). Wounded soldiers are coming in on trains. We hope to establish a hospital here in a large agricultural school building. The confusion is something beyond words. Nobody seems to know anything for certain. You simply live from hour to hour waiting for what is going to happen next. Luckily, food is cheaper here, particularly butter, cheese and dairy stuff. In fact, the cheapest I have seen. I do hope I can buy tomorrow morning something to put on the feet of these little tots. How they are going to live if they don't get some air and exercise, I don't know. Moreover, they will surely freeze to death. Thank God it is not <u>very</u> cold here tonight; about freezing I should say. I gave such stuff as I could scrape up among the staff on this today to some children that were next to naked, simply wrapped up in rags. Thank God you live in America is all I can say.

One or two things I have learned about the way the Russians live: for instance they know <u>absolutely</u> nothing about sanitation, and as for fresh air, I really believe they are more afraid of it in their houses than we would be of poisonous gases. All windows and doors are double on account of the severe cold; and they are hermetically sealed up in the fall so that there is not the slightest bit of ventilation possible. They will almost shout at you if you leave the door ajar when you come in a store or office. The stench is indescribable. It really sickens me instantly. I can understand how the men live because they are out in the fine air (the finest I know of) all day; but the women and children huddled in houses beat me.

This is a very jumbled letter as you will see; but I am just writing down things as I have time and therefore the subjects are naturally a little disconnected! After you have read it, please send it on to father as he will be interested.

Russia certainly is in confusion confounded today and if things are many times as bad in European Russia as they are in Siberia, what must they be! No one knows what is going on in Moscow and Petrograd. Last news from there months ago told a story so black that it could hardly be worse. It is hard to believe that a nation of 180,000,000 people will not work itself out into some sort of an orderly state someday; but no one now sees just how soon this will be. The peasant who forms by far the greater part of the population is undoubtedly the backbone of the country and its ultimate hope of salvation. How soon the Bolsheviks will fade away I do not know; today they are growing stronger. I am reliably told by military officials that they have an army of 68 Divisions on the Volga front. This means approximately 1,750,000 men. They are officered by Germans; indeed the army is being formed by <u>German organization</u>. I don't think they could get together such an army under their own supervision for they seem to have no organizing power of their own. I believe that if it is true that Germany is withdrawing her troops from the Ukraine, as we hear, that this Bolshevik army will soon crumble for the Germans will soon withdraw from it. But- I don't know, of course, and there are so many opinions and reports that it is absolutely impossible to get at the truth. But whatever happens militarily it is perfectly sure that this will be a dark winter in Russia; and the aid to be given to the poor and refugees will be just as great as if the war went on. I hope to get out of here <u>via Europe</u> so as to reach home in May 1919 if possible; but I cannot say at all whether this will be possible. One cannot run away and leave such a condition as long as the needs are so great. It will be years before things are back to normal again.

I am writing by candle light and I can hear little children in box-cars just outside my window crying. It is really sickening. I wish I had 10,000

Fig. 4: Railway box-cars

car loads of clothes, shoes, etc. They are needed more than anything else in the world here today unless it be medicines of which there are none. Soldiers wounds are being bandaged with rags. I shall certainly live-out a great many years of my life this winter. But things can even be darker than they are here. I have working with me a man who has just come up from Armenia and he says people are lying about in the fields, by the road sides, etc., dying by the thousands. He has crossed fields where you could hardly step without walking on them- but enough of this. I am going to bed – but how can one sleep in such surroundings. By way of diversion, and to keep my mind off such things, I am reading "Martin Chuzzlewit". They tell me the Ural Mts are full of very pretty stones and I hope to pick up some to bring home to you. I also want to bring home a Samovar which everybody here uses for heating water for tea.

Omsk, Monday Nov.11th, 7 a.m.

I have just had an awful blow. The man who has been with me and who speaks the language has received a cable to return to Armenia. I don't know what I shall do. It's an impossible handicap not to be able to speak the language; and to be left up here for months without anyone who can help me is the most gloomy prospect I have ever faced. However, there will be <u>some</u> way, I suppose. Now the time is drawing near when I shall have to close this letter for I want to send it out to Vladivostok by some Americans to be mailed there.

Now my dear, as I have so often said, there is nothing in the world that will strengthen me in my work as to know that everything at home is alright. I have had no word since October 4th, but I know you will take every care of those most dear to me. I can't tell you what I'd give to hear from you all this morning.

Fig. 5: Omsk railway station

8 p.m.

Well I think I have seen the place I am to spend the winter. It is in a large agricultural school building about 4 miles from Omsk where we are going to establish a hospital. The road leading to the school from Omsk is very much like some roads I have seen in New England. It is over flat country rather thickly grown over with a grey birch much like ours except that it is larger and does not grow in clumps but singly. I expect to walk back and forth from the school to my office in town which I hope will be in the American Consulate.

Omsk is not an attractive city. It is flat and rather run down. There are some large and beautiful churches byzantine in architecture and one or two very large modern buildings – particularly the law court building just finished.

Fig. 6: Crowds outside Omsk cathedral

Now a word to you chicks and to "Bruzz". I want to leave here about April 1st so as to be home early in May. I wish you would have mother show you on the globe just where I am. You will see that I am almost straight down under your feet. That proves the world is round. It's not cold here now, but there is some snow. Now there's one thing that I had rather you children would learn than anything else, and that is <u>to give</u> to people who are not so well off as you are. There are so many little girls and boys here that have absolutely nothing – not even a pair of shoes so that they can go out and play in the snow as you. They have been driven from their homes by this war and had to leave so quickly that they did not have time to take with them anything except what they had on their back. Their clothes are tattered into rags. Many of them had as good clothes as you one time, but now have nothing. I know you would gladly give them some of yours if you could only get them over here for them. Think of them at Christmas when you are getting your presents. I am going to buy things for them with the Red Cross money which the people in the United States gave. Part of it will be money that you and the other people in Concord gave. Aren't you glad you gave your money for such a good thing? I think of you every day and wonder whether you are enjoying school as much as ever. I do wish I could be with you for Thanksgiving dinner and Christmas. I hope you will have this letter by Christmas, but I am afraid you will not. You might try to reach me by letter c/o American Consulate, Omsk, Siberia. I may get it before I leave here for home. Give my best love to "Bruzz" who will be so grown up when I next see him that I shall not know him. I look at your pictures every day and send you lots of love and kisses in this letter.

My dear, I shall have to close for this time, but will try to get you another letter soon. You may show this one to anyone whom you think might be interested in what I am doing, but by no means let any of this get into print. How I would love to see you tonight and your chicks with you. Cheer up and do not worry. I am alright and will get home in May.

Love and kisses, Ooooo, Henry

A train load of English soldiers just coming in. Good to hear a language I can understand.

Nov. 12

Still at Omsk. We have just heard that Germany has agreed to an armistice the terms of which undoubtedly indicate that the war is over. I should give a good deal to be in the U.S. tonight. What rejoicing there must be among the people there. Think of the relief to mothers, wives, and sisters of our soldiers. The most gigantic struggle in history is over; and what a credit to the U.S.!

I do wish I could start home tonight; but, as I have said, the refugee work will be as great as though nothing had happened. Indeed the story of suffering and misery increases to an extent that is simply appalling. Thousands of lives will go out in Russia this winter in spite of all that can be done. I feel tonight the most helpless I have ever felt in my life. Helpless because there is so little I can do. I wonder if I have made a mistake in going into something that is so harrowing that it takes the life out of me. I don't see how people can stand it. I am sure I never could permanently.

If there was anyone here who could do the work I surely would give up; but I am not going to for a minute. I should never feel right again. I have never before seen such misery; and I suppose I will after a while become as doctors do: hardened to it. I know I never should. I now feel as though I never could be happy again to have so many blessings when I realise there is so much suffering in the world. It takes all the pleasure out of life and makes you feel that nothing is truer than that one half the world does not know how the other half lives. I know that you have always felt as great pity for old folks as for young; but I am much more affected by children suffering than by older persons. I always feel that it is keener. It is the sick under such conditions that simply takes the stomach right out of me. Perhaps when they are so sick they feel less the lack of comforts than when they are well. Their little pale faces pressed to the windows of their hovels when they have no clothes to go out into the fresh air and play as other children, is a sight that wrings the very heart of one.

Well, goodbye again. God bless you all with love and kisses.

Ooooo H.

Be careful of fires in the house with the chicks standing too near. H.

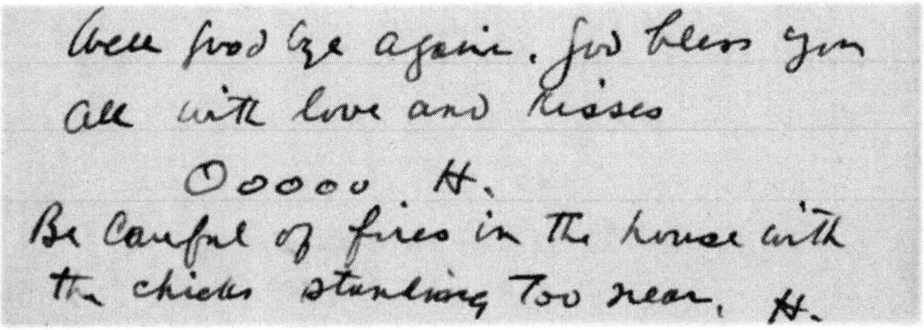
Well good bye again. God bless you
all with love and kisses
Ooooo H.
Be careful of fires in the house with
the chicks standing Too near. H.

Fig. 7: Part of the original of this letter

Letter from Omsk, Siberia
December 1, 1918

Dear Helen,

Mr. Bernstein returned here today on his way to the States because he could not get home via Europe, and I am sending this letter by him. He is the correspondent for the New York Times. I have had a most interesting day. Drove out in a drosky, 3 horses, as you see in pictures, cossack driver standing up wrapped in fur, yelling at horses and cracking whip; horses going at dead run across the brittle, white snow with six of us in sleigh. It certainly was picturesque. Stopped at a farm house in the village where we had tea. It is a Cossack village, people all prosperous or mostly so. Had chance to go over whole house and see how they live. House warm, cosy, filled with flowers. People sleep on floor mostly, though 2 narrow beds. About 10 in family including 2 billeted soldiers. House and all out buildings, barns, etc. were surrounded by high woven brush fence, inside of which was birch wood nicely piled as in New England, hay and straw stacks, sleighs, etc., everything neat; about 70 chickens, geese, hogs, cattle, fine horses. Everything as warm and tight as it could be in this cold country. Old people, man, wife and sister-in-law about 60, daughter with 2 cunning children. Saw them cook, bake bread in huge brick oven on which people sleep cold nights. Swinging bed from ceiling to hold stranded travellers and others (They pack about 10 people into space we could fit 4). People very nice, do wish I could understand the language. Showed me all about house which was big, tightly built and very warm. It was a great relief to get away for a few hours from the awful misery I have been faced with and shall be faced with all winter. How I wish everybody was as well off as these! Plenty meat, poultry, flour, but no sugar, kerosene, cloth or shoes, except at awful prices – but on the whole very well off. The horses are simply superb; and the cossacks are the best riders and drivers in the world. They go at a dead run and the horses simply love it. They are well fed. They never blanket them and after they stand for five minutes after running, they are simply white with frost. Many wolves, foxes, rabbits (Jack) and pheasants in woods.

Hope to get chance to shoot some – but no time, no gun, no ammunition! Omsk is in the centre of a great plain with no mountains to the north, so that it is open clear up to the Arctic Ocean. Hence wind sweeps down here in unbroken gales and when the temperature is low you have to be very careful or you will freeze in 2 minutes. I have already nipped one of my ears though I keep them covered most of the time – But oh! The weather is so fine; just like northern New England as its best, no wet, sloppy days – just cold, dry, sparkling snow. You can hear the sleighs screeching for miles, and they are so picturesque. If there was no misery up here due to this war, it would be an ideal place to spend the winter. I am thinking of driving in a sleigh to a city, 900 versts (600 miles) north of here. They say it can be done in 3 days! Think of it, starting from Boston to Cleveland in a sleigh! You sleep in the sleigh and they go day and night, only getting out at stations – where they change horses – to get something to eat. It will be an experience if I do it. There are so many things I want to bring you, but have not got anything yet.

I know how you would like some ermine skins and I am trying to get some - but I am so busy that I have not time to think of anything but my

Fig. 8: Omsk Cathedral with horse and carriage

work. Then, there are beautiful stones, aquamarines, alexandrines, sapphires, emeralds, etc., from the Urals which everybody takes home. Samovars also, which every Russian family has for making tea are very nice, especially the brass ones. Also fine fur coats but they are very expensive – also camel's hair shawls, etc.

December 2

The 3rd Sanitary train came in today and brought many letters, but alas! there was none but business letters for me. I told you when I left that there was no use writing me; for I then thought I should be moving about through the Orient. Still I could not but hope that you would send a letter on the chance that it would reach me. I was so disappointed not to hear from the children while in San Francisco and I can't yet understand it. Indeed I have not had a word from them since I last saw them in Concord. Still I can stand everything if I only knew they and you were alright. Things are so strange and lonely up here, and there is really no one whom I know or in whom I have any particular interest. I left all the people I knew when I left Vladivostok and some of them have already gone back and I shall not see the others again, I fear. I have a very interesting interpreter (everybody has to have an interpreter). He is an Armenian from the Caucasus and he is a gentleman. He has been in the U.S, and all over the world. He is very well-to-do and is a refugee himself. He has a most attractive little wife who speaks French very well. They will live with me until I get through up here, I hope. They are so refined and nice. I have become very much attached to them both.

I told you I was reading Martin Chuzzlewit, and really enjoyed it. There was one chapter XXVIII, the end of which made me think a good deal. Jonas Chuzzlewit seemed to me to remind me of some one – you understand, I know, but I think this person is worth saving if Jonas is not! I wonder what Rob is doing. I understand our troops in the U.S. are just being demobilized and I suppose by the time you get this letter (and my second letter, which, by the way, Mr. Bernstein is also going to take to the States to mail) all the army camps will be vacated and the boys back home at their old jobs. I wish, more than I can tell you, that I were starting back. It is an awfully homesickly feeling that comes over me when I see these men leaving for their homes in America. Don't think I am losing my courage for I am not. But I am working under unheard of difficulties and trials and things are so different from any I have ever gone through before, that it tries my patience and courage to the limit. I know everything will go on at home just as well as if I were at home or in San Francisco; but somehow I would feel almost like being at home if I were <u>anywhere</u> in the U.S. It is now late into the night and I am writing in a cold, cheerless cabin in order to get this off with Mr. Bernstein who leaves early in the morning. I think you ought to get this letter by January 20th if all goes well with Mr. B's journey. I am going to cable you again so that you will get the message by Christmas and do hope I shall hear from you by cable by that time. I must now go to bed for I have to rise early to get many things started tomorrow. I will add a line or so then, just as a parting word – so you will hear from me at least 12 hours later than now. Good night, much love and kisses to all.

December 3

Well, this is the last chance. I am feeling finely this morning, really much better than for some time. I hope you have cabled me. Now love and kisses to all. Please tell all my friends, what I am doing. Good bye, till the next time.

Ooooo Henry

Kiss every chick 10 times.

Omsk, Siberia, 3 December 1918

My dear Helen,

I have just heard that Mr. Noyes, a Y.M.C.A. man, is starting for the States tomorrow and I am hurrying off another letter to you. It may reach you even before the <u>two</u> I have sent today by Mr. Bernstein. There is really so much to say that it is discouraging to try to write it *[censored]* in the crowded barracks here I hear that the people – mostly children are *[censored, probably* dying*]* very, very fast. Poor things, at times I am glad for them. - If they could only be made comfortable in their last moments. I have so often wondered lately whether or not people who are deathly sick feel the lack of comforts as much as well – I hope and <u>believe</u> not. - The news from the front is more confusing than ever – Many think the Bolsheviks will not break up for months – and that there is no peace or order in sight for Russia. Poor ignorant people, they do not know what they are fighting for, about or at. Such chaos, disorder, confusion, misery you never heard of. It is laughable if it were not so deadly serious in its results. How, where, when, the seething mass will quiet down, no one knows. Tell Mabel and Pinto there is a chance that I may go to the States via the *[obliterated by earlier censoring]* Italy, etc. If so, I shall certainly try to visit their place. I will keep you posted by cable when I start and *[obliterated by earlier censoring]* going. This, of course, will not be for some time unless we are driven out of here by the Bolsheviks.

Dear chicks,

How you would live in this country in winter! It is so cold that you could not make snow-men for the snow is too dry; but the coasting is the finest you ever saw. The children here use the funniest little sleds made out of birch trees, very much like the birch that grow on Fairhaven Hill. They are very small sleds and the boys pick them up and run and then drop down on them and slide. The bigger boys are continually pushing and wrestling with one another, rolling in the soft snow. The dogs are doing the same. Sometimes all are mixed up together and then they make the snow fly. The children are very warmly dressed in felt boots of very pretty colours – usually red – and they all wear fur coats and fur caps pulled down tightly over their ears. Their eyes are bright and their faces red. I speak only of the children whose parents have homes and something to live on. Alas! dear children, there are many, many little ones like you in this country now who have been driven from their homes far away in the summertime and who have no clothing except what they hurried away with. Poor things, they will have a hard time this winter. Of Christmas presents they will, of course, have none. They will be fortunate if they get enough to eat and something to keep them warm. I want you to think of them when you are eating your good meals and going to your warm beds. I know you will; and that you would be glad to help them if you could. You will always get more joy out of life by doing things for people who are not so well off as you are than in any other way. I do wish you could see the beautiful horses that are here. My, but they can run fast; and for many, many miles without stopping. The strongest of them are little, stubby horses much the shape of "Pixy". They are so hardy that they stand without blankets in the very cold weather and don't seem to mind at all. People say they often get their food by pawing in the snow. - I don't know – but I do know they are fat and look perfectly happy.

December 4th *8 a.m.*

Chicks: I shall not have time to write you much more for the man is going off with the mail. I will try to get you a longer letter next time. It is <u>warm</u> enough to snow here this morning. I wish you could see how father lives: he sleeps in a small room in a sleeping car where there is hardly enough room to turn around – about the size of our telephone closet and I eat in a freight car! You would laugh if you could see the cook - he is Chinese – and the waiter is a Czech. We toast our bread on top of the stove that heats the car. We have to boil all milk and water before drinking it. I'll have some great stories to tell you when I get back.

Much love to Bruzz and kisses to all,

Father

Letter to Otis H. Cutler of American Red Cross, 3 Dec 1918

Omsk, Dec. 3d, 1918.

Otis H. Cutler,
    American Red Cross,
        Washington, D. C.

My dear Mr. Cutler:

        I have just time to send you a note by Mr. Bernstein, who is leaving Omsk today for the States. So many things have happened since I last wrote you in this big wide world that I hardly know what to say first, so I am not going to say much or anything.

        I am wondering whether the Red Cross offices in Washington have begun to be closed down, and whether there will be another drive for funds, and how many of the old men will be in Washington when I get back.

        As I wrote you from Vladivostok, I decided after I arrived in Siberia to engage in the work with the refugees, and that job I am now hard at. It would take too long and would harrow you entirely too much for me to tell you what I have seen since I last saw you. I am keeping a diary, and shall of course make a report on my work, and when I come back to the States, I hope it will soon thereafter be my pleasure to talk the whole thing over with you. I am in charge of the refugee work in Western Siberia, which includes the territory from Lake Baikal to the Ural Mountains. Hundreds of thousands of refugees have poured over these mountains driven by the Bolshevik forces, and are quartered in dug-outs, friehg cars, and every sort of covering they can find along the railway lines. I can leave to your imagination the conditions under which they live. Temperature 0 - 40 below.

        You know how much I know about refugee work, but I am going to stick it out until March 1st at the latest, and do everything I can to help.

        I am so grateful to you for the interest you have shown in getting my messages to Mrs. Thompson and hers to me. You know that I appreciate it. Please give my regards to everybody I know in Washington and New York, and believe me most sincerely yours,

        With the best wishes of the season,

            Signed - Henry S. Thompson.

Omsk, December 6, 1918

My dear:

I can't tell you <u>how</u> happy I am tonight at receiving a cable from you saying that the family are fine and that you have written to Vladivostok. I don't know whether I shall ever get your letter; but I <u>do</u> know that I have now heard from you and that you were all well on or about December 1st. Just remember this means the first direct word I have had from you for <u>2</u> months; for the last telegram was dated October 4, and that means it must have left you about October 1st. The mail conditions here are simply deplorable. I shall be interested to check up when I get back to see how many of my letters you have received. I am numbering my letters now so as to know. Yesterday, I wrote you and the chicks a joint letter which I hope you will receive.

Still I am not badly off compared with many, many German, Austrian and Czech prisoners with whom I have talked every day. Many of them have not heard from their families since the beginning of the war – 4½ years ago. Poor things, if you could only see their faces! How anxious they are and how tired of this awful war. They are so glad to have anyone talk with them. There are many of them educated, refined men – and they are now an awful sight. Occasionally they speak English and I can make myself understood in German well enough to carry on conversation with them. I have a great many working for me every day, and they <u>are</u> such good, thorough workers, and so respectful. My heart goes out to the poor wretches; and they have so often told me that their comrade prisoners have died of cold and starvation here in Siberia on the railway lines. They always ask me how soon I think they will be allowed to go home. Alas! I cannot tell them. I think the collateral and indirect misery of this war is even greater than the direct. Somehow I can stand seeing the wounded men on sanitary trains and hospitals much better than I can the poor, suffering, homeless women and children and old and sick. It will take a generation to get all this chaos and confusion straightened out. Can you wonder they lose their <u>morale</u> and courage? I am sure you would not if you saw but half of what I have seen. I do hope you have been (I don't know what I intended to say for it was 2 days ago when I started to write that sentence. It is <u>now</u> Sunday evening December 8ᵗʰ). This has been one of the grandest days you can possibly imagine. Still, bright, clear, sparkling with snow; so warm that one could walk out without any overcoat. If you look at the map, you will see that there is a great river, the Ob, running through this town (or rather the town is on the river!) It

Fig. 9: Woman washing clothes in an ice hole

is about as wide as the Charles at the basin. It has, of course, been frozen over for a month or so and is crossed many places by roads so that it is a regular highway. It was covered with sleighs today and there was some skating and skiing. People get a large part of their water from the river and there were hundreds of holes cut through the ice. They also water their horses and cattle through the ice. Whatever else one maligns Siberia with, it certainly cannot be about her weather. It has been the most perfect article I have ever seen since I arrived here. I imagine that it grows monotonous after <u>6</u> months; but it certainly is fine for a while.

I do wish we could get some news of what is going on in the world. We know absolutely nothing here except scraps we pick up. We do not know <u>definitely</u> that there is to be <u>peace</u>, but we judge so. I do wish they would quit their fighting so that thousands of refugees could return to their homes. The situation here is ludicrous; the Czechs are fighting the Bolsheviks; yet what for? They have nothing to gain as their country is to be free. Yet if the Czechs withdraw from Russia the Bolsheviks will overrun the place for the Russians are not organized nor do they <u>want</u> to fight. It looks very much to me as though the Czechs are being used as a cat's paw. I can't see what in the world they have to gain by fighting these wild revolutionists. They are having little or no help from this side by the Allies. Where it will end no one knows. I hope it will be settled by the end of February as I want to get through to Europe at that time.

I do wish I could give you a picture of how we are living. Our car is in a big freight yard and gets banged and pushed about every day. There are hundreds of cars of troops, horses, guns wagons, supplies, refugees, etc., etc., in the yard all the time. You never saw such a sight or heard such a noise. On one side of my car are the cars with the horses of the 25th Middlesex. They stamp and paw all night, poor things. They have not been out of the cars since I came here a month ago. On the other side are a train load of French who are the jolliest crowd I ever saw. There are 1000's of cars of Russians – packed in box cars. I do not believe they get a chance to sleep – living in indescribably dirty surroundings. Then there are the refugees who scramble out of cars running under and over the cars

Fig. 10: Families in railway box car

to the hot water place to get hot water for their tea (if they are lucky enough to have tea). Poor things, they live largely on black bread. How the little ones survive, I don't know. Then there are the dogs of which there are 100s. They simply fill the yard to pick up such offal as they can. I don't see how they live either, but as a matter of fact, they look in pretty good condition. They are generally mongrels of every description, but they are some really very good looking dogs among them. One other thing about Russian dogs – they seem to be very good natured. I have never had one growl at me; and they are very friendly. I have not seen any driving sledges although I have heard of it. I believe I told you that in Russia, generally speaking, there are no bathrooms in the houses. There are bath houses (public) to which the people go. These are provided with private rooms called "numbers" and then a large public room. The houses are open daily, except Sundays and holidays, and, by-the-way, I never heard of so many holidays anywhere; there is at least <u>one</u> every week – mostly church holidays. I used the bath house the other day, and they are really quite good. There are about 4 different rooms to the best suites – each with a different temperature. The warmest is quite as hot as our Turkish bath houses. Everyone must bring their own soap and towels. Soap here is very expensive – and I can't see why for they have lots of wood ashes and plenty of fats; and that's all they need to make soap. Candles, too, are entirely too dear for a country where they have so much tallow. I am perfectly sure that prices are needlessly high here. I am sure – I know, in fact – there is much profiteering – there is no government to <u>regulate</u>; so they run wild.

Fig. 11: American Expeditionary Forces hospital car

December 14, 9 p.m.

I hear the Czech courier is going out tomorrow and I am hurrying up this note to forward it by him. I do hope you will get these letters. You must not think that all the refugees are poor. Whole towns and cities and villages fled across the mountains ahead of the Bolsheviki; and naturally there were a good many well-to-do people among them. You see therefore on the streets, in the restaurants, etc., many people dressed in fine furs. This to me only exaggerates the condition of the very poor. The contrast is more marked. While the refugees from each city or community in European Russia have organized themselves into more or less compact community groups here, they seem to me to be very ineffective toward rendering aid to the poor from their community. I spend hours every day trying to help them help themselves. I do wish you could hear some of the requests – they made on me when I first started to interview them <u>as to the most urgent needs among the poor</u>. Some wanted steam laundries, libraries, stores, etc. Think of this when many of their children were starving and freezing! It really is too trying; and it's a good thing they can't understand English for I certainly cursed them out roundly. I have never seen a people so full of high-sounding socialistic schemes and with so little practical sense and idea of organization. They always want to start some kind of a <u>Cooperative</u> woolen or shoe factory with about 3 officials for every 1 workman; and they cannot imagine anyone working without getting some rake-off or pay. They can't understand how the Red Cross can find people who will <u>give</u> their time for such work. They seem to me at times to be <u>fatalistic</u> or something of the kind for they are much inclined to do very little for their unfortunate. I wish you could see the Russian Red Cross <u>in action</u>. It really is a joke. For the life of me I can't see a <u>single thing</u> they do. There are about a 1000 officials all with high sounding titles and documents covered with seals to show their authority – and there are <u>no</u> workers as far as I can see.

The men sit around in their offices incessantly smoking cigarettes and the women (nurses and all) seem to me to be doing <u>nothing</u>. Of course there must be exceptions; but in this place where there is probably more real R.C. work to do than in any other spot in the world, they are accomplishing nothing. They came around and offered their services to me very generously when I first arrived and although that was a month ago and I gave them plenty to do. They have done nothing to date.

One of the matters that is worrying me somewhat now is the way I am exposed to typhus. There is an epidemic of it here and while I am supposed to be immune to smallpox and typhoid of which there is much, there is as you probably know no vaccine for typhus. It is carried by the body-louse which is very prolific in the dirty – barracks where these people live. I am- in spite of all precautions naturally much exposed to the bug – and though I cover myself with kerosene, I constantly dread the thing for it would go very hard with us I fear if we got it. It does not generally prove fatal with the Russians for they are apparently somewhat immune; but I hear it always goes very hard with foreigners. I hardly have time to worry about it, but it sometimes gets on my mind very much. I will be careful. Don't worry. Now I must stop for they are yelling outside my cabin.

Be careful - Many kisses and lots of love to the chicks and all and much for yourself. Keep count of the letters to see if you get them all. I wish I could have seen the faces of about 1000 little tots I gave boots-clothing, etc. Nothing gives me more joy.

Love, Ooooo Henry

My dear, I am numbering these pages 5a, 6a, 7a, 8a, 9a, 10a, 11a, 12a, for they are meant privately for you. I thought you might come to show or send the rest of my letters to father, Charlotte, Mabel, Esther, etc. and you can do so without showing these pages. I want you to send my letters to father.

Now, my dear, there is not one single angle of the possibilities of your state when I left you that I have not thought out; and today I do not know what the possibilities are. I have assumed that next May another little one would come into our home; and this assumption has been strengthened by the words in your cable saying "have written Vladivostok". How I await that letter I cannot tell you; and how small the chances of my ever receiving it are! I am using every precaution to have that letter get to me, and I have almost decided to go back 5000 miles to Vladivostok to get it. Indeed, upon it depend my plans. If you want me home (as I certainly want to be if anything is to happen) I shall have to change my plans and come home <u>via</u> the West, i.e. via the Pacific. If you do not need me, I want to go home <u>via</u> Europe so as to see some of the great battlegrounds. If I come home <u>via</u> Pacific, I may decide to go back to Europe after your party is well over as I certainly want to go to Europe and there will be as much if not more work to do there now as during the war. I shall therefore await with great anxiety the arrival of your letter – if it doesn't come by March 1st, I shall cable you for instructions.

I know, dear, how much you want another little mate for "Bruzz". Of course I should like one, too; but I can never tell you the anxiety I have gone through since I left you on account of the time we may expect him. I have wished, oh so many times, that I could receive word that there was "nothing doing". Nothing would make me more easy just at present; but if the worst! is to happen there is nothing to do but to make the best of it. I know you will be alright; and I thank God that Rob got safely back for I know that took a great burden off your mind. If there is any thing in 'prenatal influence' and I believe there is, I could hardly imagine a more inopportune time to venture on motherhood. But I know your happy, cheerful nature will go a long way toward offsetting the worries incident to the present time. I can honestly report a <u>very much</u> improved state of health for myself; and although I am living under conditions both as to be exposed to disease and lack of comfort such as I have never experienced before, I have a firm belief that I will pull through alright. <u>Do not worry about me</u>. I know you will not. Two and a half months will see my term of service ended unless unexpected emergencies arise and I feel perfectly clear in my conscience that I have "done my bit", and ought to be released after March 1st. What I am to do after I once get back I do not know. I think much of farming or perhaps secretarial work. I doubt much whether I shall ever go back into <u>strictly</u> business again though I <u>may</u>. I am beginning to feel the effects of many years of hard work; and the last six months have taken a great deal out of me so that I get tired very easily. I shall take a good rest when through and shall soon be myself again. I wish I knew how Phil Cabot is. He has been the best friend I have and I have begun to appreciate how really few <u>reliable</u> friends one has in this world. Phil's health worried me greatly. Poor fellow, he has allowed his introspection and high nervous temperament to eat his life out much earlier than he should have. He felt when I left him that we should never see each other again, <u>but I didn't</u>. I have thought- many, many times lately of what my life has been for the last <u>eleven</u> years. There is so much of it that I would erase – so much of it that has been anything but happy when it should have been nothing but happiness, that I come to the conclusion that is has been wasted – and the fault has been <u>entirely</u> my own. My own suffering I could forget; but it will be hard to make amends to others for the suffering I have caused them. At times it seems almost useless to try at this late date. Now to return to something more cheerful – what do you think of our somewhat casual suggestion of trying our luck with Mabel and Pinto? At times it has seemed to me almost visionary; and again it has seemed as though it might be a possibility. The really serious objection to the plan, I think, is that if we are to make Concord our future home, it will be entirely impracticable to try to live for the farming part of the year at Newport and the rest at Concord. Farming, like any other business, cannot be run at long range; and it would mean that we should be obliged to live at Paradise for at least 9 or 10 months of the year or else I personally would. The schooling, house and other problems would be very complicated. I have come to love Fairhaven Hill and Concord. They have sad as well as happy memories for me which make me cherish the place equally for both. I can't bear to think of a change; and I don't like the idea of living away from the place for the greater part of each year. Mid-summer is really the only undesirable time; and for that a sojourn at the shore is better than 9 months absence. However, will talk this over later. I still hanker after Squibnocket; but there too, it would practically mean leaving Concord; or at least <u>my</u> continued absence for the greater part of the time. If I could find a farm that I could handle within striking distance of Concord - that is, one that I could go out to daily from Concord, I might work something out of that. I have no misgivings about making anything but a <u>living</u> out of a farm; but I feel sure I can make that. I really expect I shall settle down to some secretarial job – perhaps with the College – and pass the remainder of my days in Boston and Concord. The last 4 years have had so much that was unexpected and new to me that no one knows nor do I venture to predict what the next 4 will bring. I only hope it brings the opportunity to be more with my family – this I <u>must</u> have if I have to take them with me. It's too much of a sacrifice to miss so much of their young lives. I have had my fill of that already. I get so tired of not seeing them that I sometimes feel I could not stand it another day. Well, now I've dribbled on to you here for almost 8 pages and I suppose you are tired, so I will stop for this time as soon as I have filled this page. How I miss you dear is beyond words. If it were not that I am so busy all the time never knowing what is going to happen next, I could not stand it. I wonder if you ever think of me and whether we are thinking of each other at the same time. It is now 6 p.m. here and that means 6 a.m. with you. I picture you asleep on the upper porch. How I would love to slip up and give you a kiss that would would waken you! How surprised you would be! I have often thought that the next time I come home I would slip in on you without notice and see how I would find you all. Well, I wish that were to be tomorrow morning; but it won't be for many a morrow. Until that time, keep the dear ones well and give them piles of love and kisses, keeping for your own dear self all you can stand.

Ooooo   Henry

Letter from Omsk, Siberia
December 17, 1918

My dear Helen,

This has been the coldest day we have had: about 35 degrees[2] below zero – but I do not mind such days if the wind does not blow. Really it is wonderful: the trees are covered with frost and every breath of the horses freezes on the harness or hair and the heads of the people look like great snow balls for their breath freezes and covers the fur caps and shawls which they wear. I walked about 12 miles today and never felt better; but of course had to keep nose and ears well protected. The Russians do not wear woolen underclothing: in fact I think they do not all wear any; but such as have it, have only cotton. Another thing about the Russians will interest you and that is they seem to have a wonderful control of their tempers. The missionaries, with whom I work, and who have lived in the Orient for years, tell me that the Koreans, Japs, Chinese, etc. will lie, cheat, steal, and even murder, but you can never exasperate them to the point where they lose their tempers. They consider that entirely beneath their dignity. I wonder how this strikes you? I surmise that you have often wished I had a little oriental blood in me; or at least you would think my service in Siberia were not a total loss if I could acquire at least this one of their characteristics! How about it?

December 18, 9 p.m.

This has been a very cold day- 53 below zero – but so still and quiet that I have not felt it much – yet we have been greatly inconvenienced in our cars – water freezing cars, so cold that we have to eat with overcoats on. I have eaten all of my last meals standing. I eat only "prostoquash" - cold sour milk – and dry bread with a cup of cocoa. It is all I can stand. Three meals a day. Never have I roughed it where we had so little comfort. I wash, brush my teeth, and shave from the water I can put in

---

[2] *Thompson invariably specifies temperatures in Fahrenheit.*

the screw cup from the top of my thermos bottle, i.e. about ½ teacupful! I really have begun to count the days till my service will be through – a little over two months. I really feel I have done my share. Both the other men who came over with me have given up and gone back to America. I am determined to hold on till March 1st unless something happens and calls me away sooner.

December 19, 6 p.m.

This is a holiday here – St. Nicholas day – there are more holidays than working days and there are twice as many now as formerly for a part of the crowd still recognize the old calendar which is 13 days later than our calendar; and some are changing to our method of reckoning. If I repeat a great many things in these letters you must forgive me for I can't remember from time to time what I have written. So much comes into my mind and vision these days that I have forgotten half I ever knew. I really believe that if I were suddenly dropped down tonight into the peaceful village of Concord I should not know half of the people – or at

Fig. 12: Injured Russian soldiers

least would not be able to call them by their names. It takes pretty severe experiences to drive things out of one's mind, but I have had them during the last 3 months. A new horror has turned up here which almost puts all others in the shade, and this is the returning Russian war prisoners from Germany. Of all the possible sights you could imagine in your much troubled dreams these are the worst – starved, freezing, naked, crowded like cattle into cold box cars, they present a problem that will have the darkest history of all the tragedies of this war. I know of one train load of about 800 where over 1/3 died within a few weeks. These poor wretches were in prison camps in Germany when the Armistice was signed and their guards simply left them and they beat it for Russia. Now you can imagine, with the disorganized state of the R.R.s in Russia, with Bolsheviks in control of most of them, what chance 1,000,000 men had to get home. No money and passing through a part of the country where there was no food, they had, I think, about ½ a chance to get to their homes. Poor things, most of them have families that they have not seen for 4 years and I honestly believe ½ of them will never see their homes. I am told by a Y.M.C.A. man who has followed them, that at least 750,000 died in the prison camps in Germany, literally starved or died of typhus. I wish you could see just for <u>one minute</u>, the crowd that are without my car <u>now</u>. It is 36 below zero, nearly everyone is coughing – their feet are tied up in great bundles of straw, their clothes are burlap bags, and they are huddled together like animals awaiting transfer to another car. It's no use to try to tell you of it. You just can imagine it. Then there are the Austrian German prisoners here in Russia. I have numbers of them helping me every day – doing all sorts of things – and doing them <u>very</u> well. It has been too cold for them to do outside work for the last two days for they are not properly clothed. One of my workers has just come in to tell me she has had her pocket picked losing all her money – passport, etc. Such things happen every day here. Indeed it is unsafe to walk out after dark for you are very likely to have all your clothes taken from you by robbers. They are keener after clothes than anything else and many a person has been found robbed of all their outer clothing. Of course there are no police. There isn't any order of any kind here and it's a matter of "every fellow for himself and the Devil take the hindmost". As I have so often said if it were not for so much misery the job of staying here would have its attractions to adventurous spirits. Naturally among such a motley gang as live about these towns, there is a large number of the most desperate characters – vultures who live on the misfortunes of others, robbers, cut-throats, etc. It is a wonder to me every day how we really live where there is so little organization and order. I don't believe any human could stand six months of the life I am living here. From 7 a.m. till 12 o'clock midnight, someone is in my small cabin telling me of things that must be done at once. I cannot go to sleep after I do turn in because of the number of things on my mind and between all this and the shifting of the train there's very little chance of rest. I really think I will have to move into a house if it's possible to find one though there is not much hope as I have been looking now for over a month. You just ought to see the houses here – there is not a room that hasn't every single soul that can breathe living in it. The City Government simply goes to your house and orders you to take so many people and tells you how much rent you may collect from them. People who have nice homes here are simply furious at having people forced upon them in their parlours, kitchens, hallways, etc., but there's nothing else to do. Incidentally, I think the refugees who live in these private houses are almost worse off than any others for they tell me they are treated shamefully by the owners of the houses who are provoked at having them there. They tell me that they, the owners, will not let them heat the milk for their little babies or do anything. It certainly is an indescribable mess. Just remember, that of the 600,000 people now living in Omsk, about 450,000 are refugees!

December 20.

I think I have told you already that the refugees, generals, military critics, citizens, women and all have picked out you and Helena as the <u>beauty spots</u> in the family. Indeed I have had many small children tell me that you looked like a queen! and older folks here have said you looked as though you belonged to the royalty! I do wish you could see all the places where I have exhibited the photographs. You cannot imagine how little tots I have held on my knees have admired and played with the case. Poor things, they have no play things; and the bright-silver case attracts them at once. Children are alike the world over. There is one little, brown eyed Cossack girl that waits on me in a sort of milk depot whom I should like to bring home. She is an orphan; and about the size of Mary. I have given her warm clothing. She is really beautiful, and says she will go to America with me! Poor duck, she sleeps on the floor of a kitchen with her old grandmother. No mattress, only one blanket; earns enough to keep both – or rather earns all both have to live on – what chance has she in the world.

December 21, 1918

Today I had my first real experience in Russian hospitality. I went to a factory to buy boots for refugees and after the business was finished, the managers took me to their rooms which adjoined the office. The rooms were very comfortable – with a settee, piano, many flowers, pictures, etc. We had tea and cakes with wine and vodka, cold fish and bread, cigarettes, bon-bons, etc. They gave me a fair example of how the best class – rich class – live here. It was not bad. When the repast was over they sent me to my car – about 4 miles – with one of their best horses. Real genuine hospitality. Both young, unmarried men and very nice. I wish Sam Hoar could have dropped in. I should give a good deal to know what he would have thought of it. The Russians are much more formal and polite than we. Some believe them less genuine. I don't know – but will give them the benefit of the doubt.

Sunday morning December 22.

I wish this letter could take the flight of light so as to reach you before Christmas; but you'll have to take my thoughts instead, for indeed you'll be lucky if you ever get any of these letters. That's what makes it so hopeless to write them. I don't see why, but I have no faith that they ever get out of this country. I telegraphed to Vladivostok to see if your letter had been received. The replied no. Letters are given to couriers or anyone who is going out or coming into this country and I fear most of them feel little responsibility! I don't want to leave here until I get word from you. I don't yet know where I shall have my Christmas dinner; probably at the hospital, but it is so far away that I may not have time to get out there. I have just been thinking that this will be the first Christmas since we were married that I have been away from home. Am I right? Certainly I have never been so far away from home before. Look on the map. I could hardly be on the Earth anywhere and be farther away. When I get home, I will tell you some of the unnecessary difficulties I have in running this job. My whole force, except the prisoners, a few Austrians and Poles, are

Fig. 13: Red Cross workers

American missionaries; and of all the petty jealousies, smallness, lack of cooperation, etc., I have <u>never</u> seen the equal. <u>Every</u> night after a hard day's work, I have to sit and listen to little, petty quarrels that are too small for children. I am the ranking officer and have to settle them all; and they almost drive me wild at times. You know my temper; I am sorry to say that I have not <u>always</u> been able to keep it; but I flatter myself that I have done <u>unusually</u> well. My how I count the days till February 28 when my six months' service is ended. I am <u>very much</u> improved in health. I eat no meat, often have nothing but cold milk and hard bread. It seems to agree with me finely. I am very much interested in the daily life of these people. When they get up, what and when they eat, their beds, tables, stoves, etc., how they hitch up their horses, milk their cows, etc. etc. I am sorry I do not have time to write you all about it; but I will tell you much when I come home. (I hear you laugh.) I am reading Tolstoy's "The Cossacks Etc." which is descriptive of life in the Caucus. It is so interesting. I wish you would read it. Tell Esther I think she is right in thinking Russia will be a great field after she gets through with her 'revolting'. There are certainly commercial opportunities here far beyond any I have seen elsewhere. I am sure I could make a fortune here in a year <u>if I had American goods</u>. I spend the greater part of my time buying goods from the government – getting permission to use buildings, etc., etc. It takes more time to buy 1000 yards of cloth here than it would to buy the whole of Jordan Marsh's store. One has to see about 10 officials before you can get anything done; and by the time you have seen the last one, the first is out of office, and his authority is no good; so you have to start all over again. They are the greatest people on earth for stamps, seals, ribbons, etc., even the janitors wear uniforms; and I can't tell a stevedore from a general, so often make some beautiful <u>faux-pas</u>. The peasants, especially the Kirgish – Mongolians – are the best people here, I firmly believe. I wouldn't give house-room to the 'Intelligencia', so called. They are 'too proud to work'; and I swear I would let them starve if it were not for their poor, helpless women and children. Incidents and experiences in individual cases make the <u>greatest</u> impression on my mind. Many of such I shall never forget. I only wish I had time to write about them. This has been a rather wild day today here – mutiny broke out among a certain Russian regiment and there has been shooting going on all day. Twenty-three are known to be <u>dead</u>. Three just outside my car. I ventured out for a walk a few minutes ago and things seemed quieter. The machine guns have stopped firing and I hope we have a peaceful night. I have the car doors locked and guards at each end. The R.R. is completely tied up and my work is thus much delayed - what a country – what a people. God only knows which way they are headed. I can't write much on such subjects you know for they sometimes have a censor who reads a letter!

December 23   4:30 p.m.

Things have been popping here today. Many arrests. Martial law, etc. Can't say much. We are entirely shut in here now, the R.R. being closed both ways. There is a Dr. going out on a <u>special</u> French Consul's train and I am sending this letter by him to be mailed in China somewhere. I hope you will get it. Within 24 hours with you it will be Christmas. I hope it will be a merry one with all. I do wish I could join you instead of being here in this godforsaken spot. I hope to get some word from you for Christmas, but no word since <u>December 4</u>. I know that you are alright, but nothing helps so much as a word saying you are. Please <u>be sure</u> to send these letters to father as I positively have not had time to write but one letter. Now I must close as the messenger is leaving. I shall write a word or so whenever I have a minute and send it at every opportunity. Do keep count of the letters to see if you get them all. Give my love to everybody and lots of it to the chicks. If you can keep yourself and them happy and well till I return, I shall not worry about <u>anything else</u>.

Much love and kisses and may God keep you safe and well. Merry Christmas and a <u>Happy</u> New Year.

Ooooo Henry

Omsk, Siberia, December 24, 1918

8.15 p.m

Dear Helen,

It is now a quarter past eight in the evening here and I figure that it must be about a quarter past eight; Christmas morning, with you. What a picture I see on the hill. Mary and Helena with wide open eyes peering around the edge of the screen to see where their stockings are, and you carrying "Bruzz" in to put him down nearest to his stocking. I see the piles of packages and toys just as plainly as if they were here before me in the car; I hear the screams of delight from the girls and "Bruzz" squeezing some toy that makes a noise. What I would give to drop down from the chimney! It is really the most homesick night I have ever had. This is an anniversary of ours too, dear, and for that reason I doubly wish I were home instead of in the smallest little hole in a cold, dirty car where someone is yelling at me from 7 a.m. till 12 midnight. But I must put up with it for this Christmas and for a short time longer, and thank my lucky stars that I have a home with loved ones well off in it instead of like most of the poor wretches I work among every day most of whom have seen better days, but who now do not know whether their beloved ones are dead or alive. Oh! what a Christmas for them. I think this will be the darkest Christmas the world has ever seen; the only bright spot being that the carnage is over. In Russia that isn't true, and no one knows when light will come here. I have had a most disagreeable day – so bad that I have not eaten any supper – don't eat much anyhow – but I think I'll turn in and try to dream of you all – good night.

Christmas day – 6.30 p.m.

I went to the Consulate this morning, hoping to find a word from you, but alas! nothing doing. If you only knew how a word from you all would have been the first, most appreciated gift I possibly could have desired even if I had the choice of anything in the world, I know you would have sent one. Perhaps you did and it was delayed in transit. I know, however, you were thinking of me. I did not go to the hospital for Christmas dinner because I was too busy with Russian officials; but tonight I am going over to dine in the car of the English-American Red Cross. (These are the Philadelphia people about whom I wrote you.) If you could only peek through the window of their car. It's a 4th class Russian passenger car – that would mean a lot to you if you only could only see one of their 1st class cars. You would see a table no bigger than half the table in our living room – and one side of it is against the wall; so you can imagine how 6-six people will look seated about it! I'll write you about the dinner later as I must hurry off now so as not to keep them waiting.

9:30 p.m.

I am just back from dinner – roast goose with brown gravy, mashed potatoes, onions, carrots, cranberry sauce, bread pudding with sour cream (the latter is a delicacy with the Russians), tea and sugared bread – all well cooked, and we had quite a jolly evening. The Russian Christmas comes 13 days later than ours and we hope to have a little piece of candy for the little tots if we can possibly manage it. It will be a frightful job finding them all; but we hope to reach most of them through various committees, etc. Poor ducks, what a life they lead compared to the children you and I know. I pity them as I can hardly bear it. Good night to all.

December 26

I have just heard that another military carrier is leaving here the 29th and I am hurrying to get another letter off to you. It has been quite cold here today – about 35 below zero, but quiet, and perfectly adorable weather. There is no dust or dirt and I am as free from colds and throat affections as if I had never had any. I wear only a cotton, padded, Japanese made overcoat and am perfectly comfortable walking. I feel the cold only when I am sitting still in my car or riding in a sleigh. I am having a wonderful overcoat made by the Kirgish: both the inside and outside are strictly hand woven materials – the outer from camel's hair; and the inner from lamb's wool. I am having Kirgish silver buttons put on it. There will be nothing like it in the U.S. I haven't got it yet – and there are so many 'slips between the cup and the lip' in this country, that it is really unsafe to count on it until it is on my back.

Things are a little quieter here now, although there is still military law. No one allowed out at nights. I am never bothered – as this red cross + I wear on my military uniform is a greater protection to me than if I were covered with armour plate. I really have <u>absolutely</u> no fear of anyone purposely molesting me. The only chance is a stray bullet; and I am trying to be pretty careful when the shooting is going on. I suppose some day I will look back on these days and experiences with pride and some pleasure; but I feel now as though I would give all I have in the world to be well out of it. I am really becoming quite attached to my interpreter, Mr. Berinoff. He is so solicitous of my welfare; and looks after me in every way in the most satisfying manner. He is an Armenian and has a most wonderful business sense. This is a great help; and pleases me much.

I am becoming quite a socialist, I fear, in spite of all the bad side there is to their theories and actions. Certainly the poor people under these autocratic governments have had hard sledding; and I have great sympathy with their revolutions in many respects. They have been kept down for centuries and don't know how to act when they are freed. They will commit many excesses- and go to awful extremes – even worse at times than autocracy – but I feel after they have seen the folly of lawlessness, they will come to themselves – when I don't know. One gets such a different point of view after living with these people in these times that it ought to broaden one and make them more sympathetic.

I wish they would use sleigh bells more here – they do not all by any means use them – in fact it is the <u>exception</u>. Neither do the locomotives have bells – hence they do a lot of whistling to warn people to look out.

Two months from tonight - the 28th of February- I shall be a free man. I now have a plan of going to a large estate about 500 miles from here to stay a few weeks after I am through if I cannot get out of here by the 28th of February. I should like to see how the rich in Russia live. I will surely see it at this estate and have seen enough of how the poor live. But <u>all</u> plans are nothing but <u>plans</u>, for no one can forsee how things will be two days ahead in this wild country. Every day we have alarms about

Bolsheviki. The Bolsheviki have written me a letter asking me to take care of their children – about 8000 in number. Now how am I to do this unless I go into their territory? I am not afraid to go personally; but everyone says I would be very foolish to go as I would never get back alive. I don't believe it; but maybe they are right. I am thinking of trying it some day. Perm (look on the map) has been taken by the Czechs and Russians – and this was one of the Bolshevik strongholds.

This looks good and gives some hope of opening the way to Petrograd. I do hope it will be open by March 1st as I do so much want to go home that way. I am too tired to do more writing tonight, but will finish in the morning. I wanted to send a picture postal to all my friends, but there are none here to send. Good night.

Sunday morning, December 29 8:30 a.m.

Before I go to the Consulate for a meeting I will write you a few words. I have just arranged to give to a candy maker here two bags of our sugar out of which he will make one candy for the children. I plan to put a Christmas tree in every barracks – with some candles – and to give each little one a small bit of candy and some sunflower seed. Russians are very fond of sunflower seed and eat them as we do peanuts. I wish you could see them doing it. They put the small seed in their mouths and in some way quite skillfully crack the small seed to get the kernel out and spit out the hull all without touching their fingers to it as we do with peanuts. When you consider how small the seed is, you will see what a feat it is. Just try it. I have and can't do it; but you see the children, labourers, market women, etc. doing it all the time. The people have had no sugar to speak of for two or three years, and they are crazy for something sweet.

My only worry is I can't give them but a few pieces each; and then I know I shall miss some for it will be impossible to reach all, Poor things! My heart fairly aches for them. Some of their little brown eyes remind me constantly of the dear little one of ours, who has gone ahead. I sometimes envy her. She is happy and so much better off than most of these. Oh the tragedies of this life. - The frightful aftermath of this war. I feel the women and children suffer more than the soldiers. I am sure of it. I have so often shown the German and Austrian prisoners the picture of my own family and the tears would come to their eyes. Poor things! They love their families as much as I love mine; and I am sure I should go crazy if I knew no more of you all than they do of theirs. What surprises me more and more every day is what the human mind and body can go through and still survive. The facts are that the struggle to keep alive so occupies their minds that they cannot dwell on anything else. My respect for the sisters of mercy and men who are giving up their lives to help others constantly increases. Most people you and I know are absolutely unacquainted with what they go through. I am sure there is nothing else in life so worthwhile as to do for others. As Mamie has so often said, it is the only thing in this life that makes me really happy; and the only way to forget self. I was not made for such work. It takes too much out of me. The trouble is I can never forget what I have seen in Russia. The thought of it will stay with me forever. I wish you could see the faces of some of my Russian workers. They fairly shine with holiness and sacrifice. One sits opposite me now. What they have gone through and go through every day is perfectly inspiring. If there is any reward hereafter, they will surely come in for their share. Well now, I must quit for this time. I don't know when you will get this; but you ought to sometime in March for it is to be mailed from Vladivostok. I am so much better myself that I cannot help having the feeling that some higher power looks after me in such places. At any rate, I have no fear but that I shall come out alright – so don't worry; but count the days till I shall be with you all again.

So more kisses and love – be careful and happy and I will also.

Love to everybody, Ooooo Henry

Letter from Omsk, Siberia, December 31, 1918

11:30 p.m.

Dear Helen,

You can see from the date of this note that there is not much left of this year. If I am to make amends for my shortcomings I have but a half hour in which to do it! I can go to bed tonight – really feeling that I have tried to do something for <u>others</u> this year. Certainly more than is any other year of my life. This sounds a bit pharisaical; but you know what I mean. I mean that heretofore I have not done all that I might have until this last year. I shall not make any resolutions tonight for you know I have always been opposed to them. I shall, however, try to <u>resolve</u> that I shall hereafter in my life try to do more for other people. Before going to bed I want to wish you all the happiest new year of your lives. I only wish I were nearer to greet you. It is the new year with you and soon will be here. Love and good night.

January 1, 1919   6 p.m.

I have just heard that the messenger who was to take letter no. 7 has not yet left Omsk for the R.R. line has been cut between here and the East and no trains have gone through; so you may get this note at the same time you get <u>no. 7</u>. This has been a beautiful New Year's day here, but it has started off rather badly for me: Two of my women workers are down this morning with a high temperature and, of course, that always frightens us a bit as there is so much typhus. They are continually exposed to it and it will be nothing short of marvellous if any of us escape. I also heard by telegraph that my head worker at Taija, 400 miles East of here, was suddenly called home by the serious illness of his wife and month old baby. Then the steam pipe in our living car sprung a leak last night and here we are all frozen up and the temperature about 20 below! (Quite warm for this county). As they say, misfortunes never come singly. I just live from day to day or really from hour to hour never knowing what is going to happen next. Such a life, such a country, such a people. Mr. Berinoff, my interpreter, Mrs. B, Mr. and Mrs. Compton and Mr. Heald, YMCA workers and I slipped off this P.M. and had a little dinner together. It was pleasant to have a few hours respite. We had beef-steak, (very good, not cooked too much), potatoes, soup, and some canned cherries and vodka, which latter two delicacies we supplied ourselves! We had coffee; and cigars for the men. It was a very pleasant dinner party. When I leave Russia, I shall probably never hear of or see most of these people again; so I purposely try not to form strong friendships with them. As I have already told you, there is no one that I have met on this mission that I have become particularly interested in. I like Mr. Berinoff best of all and hope he and his wife may be able to come to America sometime to visit us. Both are very interesting; and are of the better class <u>decidedly</u>. They are refugees here, their winter home being in Petrograd, and their summer place in the Crimea. If I go home via Petrograd they will go with me that far. It looks now as though we were getting penned in here; and it may be that I shall not be able to get out either way by March 1st. But a great deal <u>may</u> and <u>can</u> happen in <u>this</u> country in two months. Last night I had my first experience looking into the business end of a loaded rifle. I wasn't scared, for it all happened so quickly I hardly knew what was up till it was all over. Luckily, I had my interpreter with me for it was dark. It is wonderful how the Red Cross is respected everywhere except among the Germans.

January 2, 1919.

I found at the Consulate this morning a telegram from Washington saying that you were all well. In spite of feeling rather badly with a starting cold, I was so cheered up with this news that I have felt more cheerful than for days. If you only knew how much such news helps, you would send me a word every month. Well now I must close for the man is hurrying off to catch the train. Keep well and cheerful and I hope you will soon have word from me that I am coming home. I do wish I had your letter. Good bye.

Lots of love and kisses, Ooooo Henry

Letter from Omsk, Siberia, January 3, 1919

10.30 p.m.

Dear Helen,

I am starting the 9th letter to you though the 7th and 8th just left today. There is a reason for starting so soon to write you again and that is that I have been laid up with a light head cold and have not left my car today. I am not really very badly off; but being a little tired and not feeling very well, I thought it wiser to stay indoors today. I have done some reading, sleeping, writing and a good deal of <u>thinking</u>.

January 4, 2 p.m.

I am really much better today but thought I would stay in for tomorrow is Sunday and I want to be entirely well by that time – my busy day. I have just received my candy back from the factory and I think it will be pretty fine for the children. The women will tie it up in square pieces of paper with ribbons at each end. I could get no bags or boxes – the ribbons or red string rather – costs $2.50 for a small spool! It will cost $40 just to wrap the candy.

Jan. 5 Sunday 6 p.m.

My dear, I can't tell how <u>glad</u> and how sad and <u>homesick</u> I am <u>all</u> at the same time; for the 40th R.C. train arrived today and brought with it your letter of Oct. 26th with the wonderful photographs of the children. They made me so homesick that I almost wept – yet so happy I was to get them and to hear from you. I am disappointed <u>only</u> in <u>one</u> piece of news – you can well guess what that was. I hardly know where to begin answering you. I had not heard of the frightful epidemic of influenza. I am thankful beyond words that you all so coped, but did hear that George Clark died of it? A letter on the same train brought the news to me from Phil Cabot. He got off – poor soul – with only a head cold which is about all the effects I have had from the same disease which is now raging among our workers here. George Clark will be a great loss to W.W. and

Co. - and think of his poor family. How very, very uncertain everything in this world is. Do be careful. Henry has grown so that I confess I could not believe my eyes: Isn't he huge? I am <u>glad</u> he is a bad fellow for you always wanted a <u>bad</u> boy (I wish you only wanted <u>one</u> boy). I had also quite a sad letter from Aunt Annie. Poor woman, she has had her share of grief, too. I wish I had time to write her a long letter; but there is scarcely time to <u>eat</u> in this country now. What wouldn't I give to be at home tonight! I never wanted so much to see you all. It is quite characteristic what you say of Helena and Mary. How different their characters are! Be careful of them till I get back. 55 days more and I shall be a free man! But the news in your letter makes me feel I <u>must</u> be home in May. This probably means returning without going to Europe-for while I think that is the <u>shortest</u> way home, if I could leave here promptly on March 1st, I feel there is little chance of going through the Bolshevik lines by that time. Such a mess you never can imagine. God only know what is going to happen next.

Rob's photograph is very good. I first thought it was taken "Somewhere in France"; but later decided it was taken on our own stone seat. I suppose Rob did not get off to France before the war was over. I hope not for Esther's sake. From all reports the farm is going on finely. Poor Bill Whitelock - he will kill himself on that farm - life is not worthwhile at the pace he is going - I <u>know</u> this for that is the way I have passed my life; and the game <u>positively</u> isn't worth the candle. I'm too old to change; but please warn him; he is so young yet! I'd give most anything if I had the disposition and temperament of a great many people I know. I see them here - they go on from day to day letting things take their course - while I simply work myself to a frenzy if things don't get done; and they <u>never</u> do in Russia! My days here are crowded so full that I have little time to <u>think</u> and <u>reflect</u> till I get into bed and then my <u>thinking</u> keeps me from sleeping; and I should literally go insane if I did not realise that there are less than 2 months more for me. I can stand it that long. I shall need about one year's rest when this job is over. I wish you were able to go off with me; but alas you will not be. I think you will find me changed in many ways when I get back. I hope all for the better. I certainly have seen more life in the last year than I ever <u>dreamed</u> could be crowded into the year. I am planning on leaving Omsk for a trip 400 miles into the Ural Mountains to see some colonies of Petrograd school children that the Red Cross has taken under its care. The trip will take at least two weeks. Do you remember Seaver Warland – the tennis player? I had a letter from him today. He is in Vladivostok for the War Trade Board; and a sicker man of his job – judging from his letters – I never heard of. I tell you one appreciates what America and home mean after they spent a month or so in this country. Nothing under heavens would induce me to stay here a year. I might like to return some day – but. How glad I am Bebo didn't come. By the way, there must be some news from his home by the time you get this letter. I hope all goes well. The weather here seems to me to be moderating very much. It hovers around zero; but really that seems warm and you soon get so used to it. I am perfectly in love with this winter climate. It is simply superb. I think, too, one could and does get on here with less discomfort than in a country where there are such changes as New England has. You soon get so you don't mind the cold; and it's always cold. It's the changes that rack the human frame. All you have to do here is to be careful on the frightfully cold days – no slop, no mud, no dampness – dry, clear, cold, bracing air day after day – it's grand beyond words. If I go on this trip to the Urals, I shall have a chance to see how the Russian aristocracy live in their estates. My interpreter who is a well-to-do man – plans to take me to such an estate. I, too, think the Osgood-Bates tragedy has probably ended as best it could for her. A bunch of 8 women and 1 man refugee workers arrived here today. Most of them are from China and Japan. They are all Americans, Poor things! Some of them are heartsick already. They will be much sicker before they get out of this country. I am constantly wondering how many of the Concord boys have returned from the camps and from the war. I suppose nearly all of those in camps in the U.S. are by this time back home. But how about those in Europe? I am so glad Sam finally got off to some camp. He would never have felt <u>entirely</u> right about it, if he hadn't. I heard that Jack joined our forces in France. I thought he would. No one wants to be left out when the roll call at home is sounded. You and Mamie certainly have done wonders in preserving fruits. I hope some of them will keep till I get home! By the way, there are no fruits up here.

In the cable I got from you on December 6, you said you had written Vladivostok. I wonder if the letter I got today is the one you referred to? At any rate, the <u>particular</u> news that I wanted was in the letter. I now know how to act. I have made this letter so personal, that I fear you will not want to send it on to father. Do as you please – but at any rate- let him know that you heard from me for I am writing no letters to anyone but you for the simple reason I haven't time. I have to squeeze in the few lines I send to you between the constant knocks at my door.

January 6, 1919 6:10 p.m.

This is Russia's Christmas Eve – 13 days later than ours. I am lying in my bunk feeling only fair – the dirty blankets – cold air – noise outside and all make anything but a comfortable picture. Still I feel rather happy for the 800 pounds of candy is all wrapped in neat ¼ pd. bags tied with red strings and ready to make about 2,400 children happy, I hope. I shall be happier still tomorrow night – when it has all been distributed. I only wish there were more of it, but it is all I could possibly scrape together. I picked up Mark Twain's "A Tramp Abroad" and have buried myself in it. It has served to take my mind off of the affairs of one of the busiest day I have spent since I came here. I ran across a curious thing in one of Twain's stories and that was my own name, Henry Thompson, spelled out plainly and clearly. It gives one a jolt to see their name in print. One sees, every time they read, other names in print; and they never wink or think about it; but to see your own makes you feel almost weird – good night.

January 7

Merry Russian Christmas! The sky is a bit overcast, but the air is sharp and cold – about 25 below. The bells have been ringing furiously all morning. Every nation makes much of Christmas – but most of them make more of a religious festival out of it than we do. Poor Russians, I am afraid this is to be a pretty sad day for most of them. There have been lost about 5,000,000 men, to say nothing of the wounded. Literally hundreds of thousands of homes have been destroyed. Untold misery and suffering prevail everywhere except in the remotest rural districts of Siberia.

What people can go through and still manage to survive is truly wonderful. Most of us have no conception of what privation means. I am glad to hear that you helped out the people in the village during the epidemic. I knew you would. It makes me shudder to think of the risk you ran.

Christmas Eve –

I did not have time to go out and help distribute candy today and I am glad I didn't; for the touching stories the women told at dinner would, I am sure, have made it an ordeal that I could not have stood. Let's hope these unfortunates will never have to go through such another Christmas. I have had a busy day with the 8 new refugee women workers that just arrived. Preserve me from ever having to work with women. One doesn't want to do this - the other doesn't want to do that. This one can't get on with so-and-so and so-and-so can't get on with somebody else. Can't you see me struggling to keep my temper - 55 days more and I shall be through. I had to find room in my already crowded dining car- (box-car) for 11 more; and what is worse still some place for them to sleep in a car that is already full and every pipe frozen up with the mercury 25 below. They are piled six deep in some beds and, poor wretches, I can hear them now groaning. - You really can't imagine how we live. Just remember, since October 24, I have not seen a bed - I have slept <u>every</u> night in a car – have forgotten what a pillow or sheet looks like – have washed, shaved, bathed and drank out of the top of a thermos bottle. Now, men can stand this for a while; but how these women put up with it puzzles me. I have so often wished I were a Dickens so I might describe and picture to you the different characters I have working with me. They are really fine women – but there are among them some awful cranks who growl from daylight to dark. (I can hear you say that this is a good experience for me; but, believe me, it has not improved my temper or my nerves.) I suppose some day I shall look back on it with a kind of satisfaction – but I am dead sure I would not go through it again unless <u>absolutely</u> necessary, for a world.

I think that if there was a flying machine leaving for the U.S. on the night of February 28, I should be inclined to take it. I am getting rid of every single thing I own so as to make my baggage as light as possible. I have just one suit, two or three handkerchieves, etc. You remember that I did not take with me any of the things I am attached to; so that there is no sentiment in disposing of them – only one shirt which Mamie gave me for Christmas, last (Viola flannel). It was always too big,-and I know she will not care. I see it every day on the back of my Armenian interpreter!

Good night and love to all.

January 8 5:30 p.m.

This has been a <u>very</u> cold day here – the coldest – it seemed in our car yet – 40 below. It is a holiday here. The Russians have 3 holidays in succession – Christmas, and the two following days. This afternoon, as I did not feel quite up to working, I went out and distributed about 100 packages of candy to the people living in box cars. Will you believe it when I tell you that I did not see hardly one of the 100 children with anything on their feet. Many of them, when the news spread that I was coming, ran down the wooden ladders that lead up to the cars, in their bare feet! Now just think of it! I went into about 50 cars, and I do wish I could picture to you the inside. I can do no better than to let you imagine how much you would get on with your family living in an American box car – then remember the Russian car is only about ½ as long. In the cars there is nothing but boards put across the cars for beds. People lie on these often without anything under them. Coal, wood, all their living utensils, stove, etc. are there of course; and the floors are dirty and cold. Such conditions you can't even imagine, you have to see them. My how happy the small ones were to get the little red and blue packages of candy; and most of them thanked me and bowed down almost to the floor. I am living in a world the like of which I never dreamed existed. -

Fig. 14: Canadian troops board the "Empress of Asia"

The Canadian soldiers have begun to arrive here. Today I saw many of them well groomed and fitted out for arctic work. We hear tonight that the Japs are to come over into Western Siberia and are to cross over into Russia and fight the Bolsheviki. I don't believe half I hear. We have had absolutely no news from the U.S or Europe lately. I have no idea what is going on at this all important time. History is being made fast and I know nothing whatsoever of the trend things are taking. I might as well be in the middle of the south sea. I hear of no messenger going out soon, so I won't write more tonight.

January 9, 8:30 p.m.

I have just finished reading Stevenson's "Across the Plains". In the last essay - "A Christmas Sermon" I ran across the lines that I have always liked so much.- They are on a card in my room which Louisa McCrady once gave me. - They begin with "To be honest, to be kind" and end with "here is a task for all that a man has of fortitude and delicacy". Aren't they fine? Look them up if you haven't them nearby. I really believe that the heavenly weather with which this country is blessed will in years to come so efface all the sadness, confusion and misery which I have seen here as to leave only the pleasantest memories of the country. It is so lovely as to be simply heavenly. How you would enjoy it. We must some winter go up into Canada where we can get a taste of it. It's so clean and fresh and sharp that one feels like jumping out of their skin all the time. I walk to and from the Consulate daily just drinking it in. I shall miss it when I go. We have just heard of the death of T. Roosevelt. A great American. How much he lived and now, perturbed spirit, it is all over. He certainly lived <u>more</u> than any other man in modern times, and did more too. I am afraid his last days were not altogether happy. He showed great fortitude and bravery in the death of his son. He had great confidence in his country – though not always in its leaders. He will, I believe, go down in history as one of the greatest and purest of Americans. Good night for today!

January 10

This has been the warmest day we have had. It is spitting snow. It is the first day I have perspired in walking to the Consulate. It really isn't warm, but only relatively so. We heard today that General Guida, who is head of the Czech Army, is to take charge of the Russian army and that vigorous efforts will be made to open up the line to Petrograd <u>via</u> Valogda. I certainly hope they get through by March 1st; but the way things go I very much doubt if they will. I am rather betting on coming home via China and Japan. If I do, I shall try to have time to run down to the Phillipines. I <u>do</u> wish your party were not scheduled for May. I should like about two months longer. I wish I had your letter. I have started to read the "Decameron of Boccaccio"! I know you will be surprised at my taste in literature! But up here it is a choice of evils! Not a choice I would make if I had the Concord library to choose from. Perhaps the wide range and varied authorship will be broadening.

I don't like to waste my time (or rather spend it) reading when I am travelling and can see things. Seeing is far the most instructive learning one can have. - I believe I have told you about the great numbers of soldiers there are drilling in Russia. They drill to singing: and it is a sound you can hear any time. There are big fields in which they manoeuvre; and you meet companies of them in the streets everywhere always singing – poor things. They seem almost too stolid to appreciate their condition and move on like a machine. There is absolutely nothing so cheap in this country as <u>life</u>. That is <u>literally</u> true. Men are treated worse than animals; their life and health sacrificed without (apparently) any regard to the fact that they are human. Well, I hear that a military messenger will leave Omsk tomorrow, so I will close this letter in order to get it off by him. If you get these letters as often and as regularly as I write them, you ought to be pretty well informed about my doings. I only wish you did; but I shall be glad if you ever get them. By the time this letter gets off, I shall have started no. 10.

Now good-bye – lots of love and kisses to the chicks. Keep them safe and well and be particularly careful of yourself.

Ooooo Henry

Fig. 15: Soldiers marching in Omsk

Letter from Omsk, Siberia
January 14, 1919 O.S.
January 1, 1919 N.S.

Dear Helen,

This is Russia's New Year's day: and it is the coldest yet, 58 degrees below zero. The cold is simply fierce. We can't keep warm in this old car – we are all on the move to keep from freezing. (The blotting paper made here in Russia is just like a board.) Last night, I went to a party – the first night I have been out to stay or do anything but work since I have been here. I slept on a couch in another man's room covered with 2 overcoats. It is the first night I have slept outside my car since October 24 when I left Vladivostok. I wonder where the next strange bed I sleep in will be? Well, as to the party, there were 8 of us: Mr. and Mrs. Berinoff, Mr. and Mrs. Compton (Y.M.C.A.), Mrs. Cherington, American Vice Consul, Mr. Giani, an Italian and his fiance and H.S.T. We went to the theatre and saw a play called the "Road to Hell". It might as well have been the road to any old seaport – so far as I could tell. The acting was melodramatic and poor. The audience was well behaved and looked intelligent. After the theatre, there was supper and dancing, all in the same building. For supper, we had good steak, good broiled mutton, with fresh sliced onions, - some cakes, a little wine and coffee finished the repast. The dancing would have amused you. The dancers whirl around like a whirling gig; how they keep from getting dizzy, I don't know. The music was good. At exactly twelve we all stood and drank. It was Mr. B's 38th birthday, so was a double celebration for him. On the whole we had a pretty good time; but it is so cold here that there is no comfort in doing anything. There are no comforts whatsoever: and that takes all the pleasure out of doing anything. I nowadays do not marvel at how <u>many</u> comforts we have in America, but at how really <u>few</u> one needs to exist. You can't appreciate how few we have and I can't explain in a letter.

January 16, 6 p.m.

This is the first chance I have had to continue. It has been fiercely cold, hovering around 50 below all the time. I tell you when the mercury gets down there and the wind blows, you have to take the greatest care not to freeze. One has no idea how quickly you can freeze. Your nose will turn white in 3 seconds almost. Of course, you have to keep your ears covered all the time up here and your face and nose most of the time. But I simply enjoy it immensely. It's the greatest joy I have walking about 6 to 8 miles every day. I don't think I could stand the strain of 12 hours work a day under such conditions as we live if it were not for the exhilarating effects of this glorious climate. It's moonlight now, and that adds to the gorgeousness. Last night, I went out about 10 p.m. to see a train of refugee workers off and the beauty of the night was simply indescribable; you could easily read a paper; and so still and quiet; every step made a screeching noise and the snow sparkled like diamonds. My, how I should love to live in such a climate <u>if I only had some comforts of home</u>. They have a great skating rink on the river here lighted by electricity and a house built on the ice for people to warm. I have not seen them skating much, but what I have seen does not impress me as much as the skating I have seen in Canada or even in New England. They use long, turned up skates much like you see pictures of in Norway, etc.

January 17, 6.30 p.m.

I will try to squeeze in a few lines before dinner. This has been a cold and busy day, colder than busier. I have a hard time to get to sleep after such days. Last night I began a new book, "Pietro Ghisleri", by Marion Crawford. I should not have chosen it if I could have had anything I wanted, but I am unable to find any other book on the train. It starts off fairly interestingly and is the only book of his I have ever read. I'll report later my final criticism.

I have failed to get my fancy overcoat – couldn't get from the Kirgish the kind of lining I wanted. I shall keep the camels' hair outercloth and may find something in China or elsewhere to line with. All I think of is starting for home. I am really getting much worried about the situation.

There are so very, very few workers here and the work is growing so fast that I know every possible means will be used to prevail on me to stay. I must insist however on going. I have good and sufficient reasons; and I do not feel the slightest pangs of conscience about not having done my part – and I have many times given them fair notice. It will be only because they cannot get others to come that they will want me to stay. I have frozen my chin and one ear a little in spite of my precautions – nothing serious. It's so hard to prevent it. I can't see that the political situation – which I have never said much about – is changing for the better – chaos reigns supreme. One can't tell from one day to the next what is going to happen. Soldiers of all the allies as well as prisoners of all the enemies are here thick and such conditions as the latter live in are such that you would never believe me if I told you them. I would give a good deal to be able to forget it all forever. Some of it will haunt me for the rest of my life. I am going to send this letter out by a messenger (military) leaving here tomorrow so must finish it up for tonight. If you get it in two months, which I doubt, I will by that time be in China or the Phillipines if I go home that way.

<u>Dear Chicks</u>: How would you like me to bring home a little brown-eyed Cossack girl about 12 years old to play with you? She is so cunning and sweet. You could not understand her language nor she yours, but she would soon learn yours. She has no father or mother and she <u>now</u> works for the Red Cross tying up bundles. She has to work every day to buy food for her old grandmother who lives with her in a poor kitchen where she sleeps on the floor. I have given her many Red Cross clothes and oh how thankful she is! I first found her waiting in a cold restaurant where she worked 9 hours a day. She is much better off now and she thinks the world of your father and says she wants to go home with him! I think I can't bring her, but I should like to bring you a photograph of her. Father hopes to start home in about forty days. I count the days as you children used to before Christmas. Give my love to "Bruzz" and tell him to be good till father gets home. Much love to you all and a great big kiss for everybody.

Good bye for this time. Ooooo Father

Letter from Omsk, Siberia, January 19, 1919

9 p.m.

Dear Helen,

I just learned at the Consulate today that letter No. 10 was put into the regular Russian mails. I have great despair of its ever reaching you. Luckily, I shall know sometime. Only about 39 days more and I shall be on my way out of this country. I wish we could get some news. We hear rumours – first that Wilson has <u>not</u> left the States – that the U.S. has withdrawn from the Peace Conference – that war has broken out anew – that Bolshevism is rampant in U.S., etc. etc. All fabrications, I believe. But how do I know? The latest newspaper I have seen from the States was dated very early in November – just after the elections. I was much surprised at some results – for instance – Walsh getting into the Senate – due I believe to the fact he was running against a weak (no pun) man! I have been picturing the children sliding down the north hill through Abbott's woods. I hope they have had a good winter for outdoor sports. This country is too level for coasting though you see a little of it. I wonder what Rob is doing? There would be a great chance for active Americans in this country if the place would ever settle down. Somehow tonight I feel a little less hopeful of Russia than ever. The people have no confidence in each other – no patriotism or love of country – scarcely any self pride – they are pretty far gone. Their attitude toward their returning prisoners, their poor, etc., is ignominious – they will let anybody, or everybody do for them and they sit by and smoke. No other people in the world would show so little guts. I often wonder whether such confusion, misery, chaos, etc., existed in France after the French Revolution. I don't think so. The French are more patriotic, provident and self respecting. Good night.

January 21 , 6.30

Just a few lines before dinner. Yesterday was the fiercest day I ever expect to see. The temperature was down to 45 below and the wind blowing. I started out from the car to walk to the Consulate but was forced to return for more covering for my face. My eyes froze shut, i.e. the eyebrows froze together instantly I got into the wind. It was the queerest feeling I ever had. But I love it. I want to tell you about the markets in Russia. They are all in the open and, of course, everything is frozen. Butter, milk and cheese are frozen so hard that milk is carried

Fig. 16: Crowds in the marketplace of Omsk

home in chunks without any vessel often; butter is packed in wooden casks and the staves are torn off and the butter chopped off in chunks. The market is full of sleighs with a kind of wicker-work bodies and these are filled with fish, ducks, geese, little pigs, pigeons, grouse, quail, pheasant, etc. all frozen so hard that people carry them under their arms, in their pockets, or strung to their belts. Whole pigs, calves, cattle are hauled to the market and there chopped up with axes on huge blocks of wood and sold. There are thousands of these animals to be seen <u>every</u> day in the market. Then there are great boxes of cranberries – the only fruit or vegetable exposed in the cold for sale. They are frozen as hard as bullets but is does not seem to hurt them as we believe it does. Our cook buys them every day; and they are really good as they are the only tart thing we get along with the great amount of fat they put into the cooking here.

```
     MEETING OF NEW YEAR BY THE AMERICANS.

               ------

        At the Commercial Club  involuntarely drew attention
   upon themselves a group of Americans noiseless  and nicely
   meeting the Russian New  Year. Among them should be pointed
   out Colonel Thompson, well known by his activity, represen-
   tative of the American Red Cross in Siberia, Refugees Relief,;
   the   Secretary of the Amer. Consulate and representative of
   the Italian Press, Faustino Giani,  the representative of
   of  the Y.M.C.A.  Mr. Compton, Vice-Consul Cherrington, the
   representative of the Press of the Capital cities,Cavalier
   of the Order   of  St.George,Mrs. Platonova-Vliaslovskaja
   and others.  Exactly at 12 o'clock  Colonel Thompson raised
   the goblet to the prosperity  and happiness of Russia  and
   expressed  his intention  to devote  all his energy  to the r
   relief of the unfortunate refugees.


              ----------

   Printed  in the paper  " Nasha Zaria " No 9 - 16th Jan.
   at Omsk.
```

Fig. 17: Translation of item from Omsk newspaper

You will remember that I wrote you on No. 10 about going to a New Year's party. Well, I was much surprised that Mr. Giani, the Italian secretary at the Consulate, made a translation of a notice that appeared in the paper – and put the notice and translation into your envelope! Now I know you will think this very vain in me, but I assure you that I did not do it. Nearly every day there is something in the papers here about me and my work; and you know how I dislike publicity. I really think the reason Giani put this notice in my letter to you was because his own name appears as you see in the notice! However, I am enclosing some copies. Just because he handed them to me today. I have been looking up the sailings of steamships for the U.S. today; I wish I knew which day I was going back. I shan't really know till I am on my way for things change every day. I would give a good deal if I did not feel that I must be back in the States.

January 26, 11 a.m.

A messenger goes out to Vladivostok today and I am sending this letter along with him. A most gorgeous day here. Sun bright – snow sparkling – about 25 below. I wish you could see and feel it. Last night after my bath at the Public bath house, I went with one of our men to the house where his mother is living and they prepared a Russian supper for us. They did not know we were coming so what they gave us was just what they had in the house – cold meat, bread, caviar, tea, cakes, vodka, etc. I do wish you could have seen us eating around the small table with a candle stuck in a bottle. The mother of the boy is the dearest old thing you can imagine. Poor woman, she has lost 3 sons and her husband in this war. She, herself, is a refugee here – having fled before the Germans. She thought her only other son (the one who went with me) was dead; and by what seems Providential guidance, he found her here in this awful place. Imagine her and his joy.

She hugged me for joy and I could not help kissing the poor old thing. (It is probably unnecessary to remark that she is the only person I have kissed since I last kissed you in Washington Sept. 4!)

She is 65 years old and will go back to America with her son as soon as they can get out of Russia.

Things are growing very much worse here and there is now little hope of me getting across to Europe. Indeed I have given it up and will return to the U.S. <u>via</u> the Orient. I hope to have time to visit the Phillipines, but that will depend on whether I have time. I do wish I knew the approximate date when you need me at home. If I do not get back till <u>May 12</u>, I shall have served the Red Cross for exactly two years. I will cable you to find out just when you need me. Well, this is all for this time. I shall <u>at once</u> begin to write letter No. 12, and then there will not be <u>many</u> more from Siberia. Much love and many kisses to all. I can hardly wait till I start back.

Ooooo Henry

Letter from Omsk, Siberia, January 28, 1919

6:30 p.m.

Dear Helen,

I am starting this letter now though I well know that letter No.11 is still lying in the hands of the courier here in Omsk. He has been unable to get a train out; and no one knows when he will leave. This is, I hope, the last letter I shall write you from Omsk for I expect within the next two weeks to leave here on my way out to the East, and down through China and to the Phillipines if I have time. I have prepared a cable to send you on the day I leave asking the approximate date when you need me at home. I am bringing with me to America, Mr. and Mrs. Berinoff, if the State Department will visa them. I have plans for him when he gets there. They are very nice people and I have come to respect and like him more and more as I know him better. They are refugees here, their property in Petrograd being in the hands of the Bolsheviki and that may mean most anything; no one knows. Mrs. Berinoff speaks French and I think you will be much interested in her. He is Armenian by blood, but of Russian citizenship. He is one of the most versatile and ablest fellows in many ways that I have ever known; and a thorough gentleman. You will like him very much. He is exceedingly handsome and everybody in the Red Cross here likes him very much. I want very much to have Rob have a talk with him because I think it would be to their mutual advantage. He comes to the States to learn something of our business ways and to establish some business connection. He will then come back to Russia. Anyone would have to be <u>entirely</u> blind indeed if they did not see the extraordinary opportunity for Americans to do a great business with Russia. She needs so many things that we have to sell. I wish I were young again. I am sure there are unusual chances ahead for both Americans and Russians if this row is ended.

January 30 6:30 p.m.

Since I wrote you last (January 28) I have had the most interesting experience I have had in Russia. I was invited by Captain (something or other) to come to his house for supper. There were 12 others there besides myself. We gathered about 8 p.m., sat and talked till eleven when we went to supper – caviar, bread, cold fish, both smoked and fresh, vodka and white wine. We ate, toasting one another – American Red Cross, Americans, Russia, etc., till 2 a.m. Then there was music and dancing, more liqueurs, coffee, tea, nuts, cake, candy – singing, etc. - all so strange. The house was a mere wooden barracks, but well lighted and warm. The people all very interesting and refined. Much kissing of hands and bowing and scraping. There was one man present who had been an attaché at the Russian Embassy in Washington – he talked in very good English – was so well read and very handsome. The women were beautiful and well dressed. When you realise that all this happened within a hundred feet of barracks where people lay dying with typhus, where many 100's of people were crowded in freight cars, and where soldiers, dogs, men, horses, trains, cannon, ammunition wagons, guards, noise, etc. were within hearing, it will give you some idea of the chaos, and how the extremes of life exist side by side in Russia. I shall never again see such life, such conditions, such people. It was after all very sad – and I could feel the restraint under which these people are living every hour. Those present were all refugees, well-to-do, nevertheless, but without homes, hopes or comfort. My God, where will it all end? You have no idea. The thing that was funniest of all was the very late hours the Russians keep in entertaining. We stayed till 3 a.m.! and I began to wonder if they would ever go home. That is the Russian way of entertaining – but I could not help feeling that they were trying to kill time. Under such conditions, life seems hardly worthwhile. Yet these people must stand by and bide their time till the light comes. What else is there to do? They can't run off, then, must make the best of things as they are. I think the well-to-do refugees really suffer more than the poor in many ways – because of the physical privations they must bear, also the mental strain which is awful. How I pity them all. It isn't living, it's mere existence. I'm glad I've seen a little of it, but I really think I could not stand it long. Good night.

February 5, 9:30 a.m.

I have just a minute while waiting to visit one of the barrack schools. My how fast the last few days have gone! I am getting ready to start down the line on my way out and there is so much to do. As the time draws near for leaving I feel sad. The life here has been so strange, so different from anything I have ever seen that it will be quite a break to leave off even though I have been at it but a short time. It's funny how one occupation chases another out of your mind: I have almost forgotten all about the business I was in before the war; and if I went back it seems now as though I would start entirely fresh.

February 25, morning

At Irkutsk on Lake Baikal (see map). It hardly seems possible that 20 days have elapsed since I last wrote. Here I am two thousand miles from where I last wrote and on my way home. I left Omsk early (12:15 a.m.) on

Fig. 18: Refugee camp

the morning of the 12th and I have never passed such a <u>sad</u> day in my life. As I looked out for the last time on the little earthen dugouts and box cars where I have seen so much misery and where there are so many faces I shall never see again, a feeling came over me too sad to describe. If I should ever come back, I fear I shall never see a great many of them for they will not all survive. I have been stopping at many points on my way out, travelling in a small service car where I have a staff of five, viz: cook, waiter, interpreter and wife and one other man. It is impossible to travel in this country without your own train. The Russian trains are simply beyond description. You wouldn't believe if I told you how the Russians travel. The RR's are very good to us putting our car off and on trains whenever we wish. The most interesting city where we stopped was Tomsk. It is the university city of Siberia. Beautiful buildings, churches, monasteries, etc. are situated in a most beautiful country on a large river. The country is much like New England – hilly and rough – covered with white birch and pine. They have a group of workers there and while there we had a good many entertainments – Theatre one night: a good play – fine stage – intelligent looking audience. Dinner parties and dances in private car of Consul General and at private houses – a very interesting week. We are now at Irkutsk which is also a fine city for Siberia. We shall not stay here long. I expect to go out tonight at 9:30. I have just received a cable from you which seems to say "Thompsons well. April twenty-nine, Helen". I think I understand it, but cannot make out what the first part means. Does it mean that others of your family are not well? At any rate I am so glad to get word and am hurrying forward as fast as possible. I want to make a hurried trip through China. I think you will probably not get this letter much before you see me for I shall not mail it until I get down into China and it will likely catch the same steamer for the States that I do. I have booked passage on the Persia Maru of the T.K.K. line leaving Yokohama April 6, but I am now going to try to find an earlier boat as this will not get me to the U.S. before April 24 and that will be close connections to reach home on the 29th. I am so anxious to get back to the States that I can hardly wait for the train to pull out. I have not the slightest idea of what is going on back there. I see the Cables from the State Department and the news sent over to the Committee on Public Information, but I read a great deal between the lines in both these sources. I have imagined very unsettled times, strikes, lack of employment, questions of what to do with returning soldiers, etc., etc. I hope we are not in for any serious disturbances. Our labouring men would, I think, not have to see much of Bolshevism to get their everlasting fill of that. I can't believe it can ever gain any headway with us. There was at least <u>order</u> with Czarism. There's nothing but murder, pillage, chaos now. How it can last – and where and when it will end no one knows. Poor Russia, poor Russia.

March 1st, 6:30 p.m. Manchuli (Manzhouli)

We arrived at this town at 7 a.m. and are unable to go further until tomorrow on account of having no engine. It is on the border between Manchuria and Siberia – looks much like one of our western plains towns except for character of buildings. It is filled largely with Chinese, but has as many Buryats, Mongolians, Russians, Japs, etc. The poorer part of the town is extremely filthy; but the better part is quite attractive. The surrounding country is <u>very</u> much like Montana or parts of Colorado – great plains with rolling hills and mountains in the distance. In the afternoon we walked up to the top of a small hill about 3 miles distant. The view was superb. There was a Japanese monument on top. There has evidently been fighting. I found pieces of shrapnel and the hill was covered with trenches and gun emplacements. I think there was fighting here between the Japs and Bolsheviki. There were also some Chinese graves with their curious offerings all about them. There were four camels grazing on the distant hill which added a great deal to the interest. I am glad to have had a chance to get out and stretch my legs after so long riding, but I was sorry to lose a day. We have had such good luck so far and we are only about 1½ days outside of Harbin where I leave my car and take the road down through China for Shanghai where I hope to sail for home.

Sunday, March 2

We have been travelling all day through Manchuria – country much like our western prairie country. It is settled largely by Chinese and the towns are spread out over a great deal of ground. It is thawing quite freely today in the bright sun. Much warmer than in Siberia.

March 3, 7 p.m. Harbin

Arrived here 4 p.m. where we will stay till tomorrow evening when we leave for Chong Chung (Changchun). There we will leave our little private car which we have travelled in since February 11 and take the regular method of travel on the Chinese Government Railway.

I am going to mail this letter at the first point I reach in China – probably Mukden (Shenyang) – and see if it gets home before I do. What wouldn't I give to be home tonight. I shall be in two months but that's a long while and there are many miles to travel.

Well keep the chicks safe till I get there and give lots of love and kisses to all. I shall soon be home.

Cheer up! Ooooo   Henry

Letter from Peking, China, March 11, 1919

My dear,

I don't know when I have been so upset as I was yesterday to get a telegram here asking me if I would not <u>please</u> remain in the work here until April 20th when there is to be an important conference in Vladivostok. I had already arranged to sail so as to be in Concord about April 20 so as to attend your party; but I have thought it all out and have come to the conclusion that I may some day regret it if I do not do everything within my power to help in this situation! The Commission from Washington and Dr. Teusler both want me to stay. I have decided to do so. <u>I would not hesitate one minute if it were not for you</u>. I cannot tell you in a letter how much I regret being away all this time; but of course everything will go off all right and there is nothing I could do if I were there. I know Mamie will look after you.

Now, as there is no use for me to try to get back to my work in Siberia for so short a time, I am going to take advantage of the chance to go to the Phillipines. I don't know when I shall ever get out here again and it seems too bad to miss this chance. I am therefore planning to leave at once for Manila <u>via</u> Shanghai and will go from Manila direct to Vladivostok <u>via</u> Shanghai and then about May 1 sail from Japan for the U.S. So I shall be home approximately one month later than I planned: that is about the <u>end</u> of May.

I am being much dined and feted here by all the very nice people who live here. There is so much to tell you about this country and its cities and people that I shall not try to do so now. There is something doing all the time, so that I do not have time to write.

I am cabling you today about my change in plans, and I do hope you will not be too much disappointed. Everybody is so sorry to delay me for <u>some</u> know why I am hurrying home. But I think you will agree that I have done the wise thing in staying. It took me a day to make up my mind.

Now, dear, do be careful and take no chances.

Much love and kisses to all of you. I cannot tell you how much I regret delaying my return.

Love, Henry Ooooo

North Ch

PEKING NOTES

(Special to The Star)

Peking, March 9th.—Colonel H. J. Thompson, of the American Red Cross, arrived in Peking this morning after a six months trip through Siberia and will remain in this city for several days before setting out on his return journey to the United States. Colonel Thompson came out to the Far East last Summer together with Major Alfred L. Castle and, after a short visit to Japan, proceeded directly to Vladivostok to assist Dr. Teusler and the American Red Cross Commission to Russia in building up the Red Cross organization in Siberia. He has been all over the country, from Vladivostok to Omsk, and is taking back with him to Washington voluminous data regarding the needs of the Siberian people from the point of view of the American Red Cross. Colonel Thompson states that the Red Cross organization is now working smoothly and doing fine work under exceedingly difficult conditions; and that the Siberian people are genuinely grateful for what is being done. The people are in need of everything that can be regarded as belonging to civilized existence; and it would take several years, given normal conditions and a good transportation system, to meet the population's requirements as to clothing, medical supplies industrial machinery and agricultural implements.

Fig. 19: Cutting from English-language newspaper "North China Star"

From Shanghai to Manila, March 16-19, 1919

Dear Helen,

Today is the 18th and we are due in Manila tomorrow morning. It is about as hot here as it is with us in July or August. It is so different from the weather I have gone through since I left home that it reminds me of the early part of last year when I was down in the tropics. I wrote the children and father postal cards from Shanghai, but did not have time to write you as I went to bed as soon as I got my tickets arranged for. I am suffering from one of the worst colds I have ever had. You remember those awful head colds I used to get nearly every winter, sometimes so bad that I had to go South to break them up. Well, I have one of that particular variety and it is most trying. I first caught it on a trip out to the Great Wall. It was a warm day, and I got warm walking then cooled off. I have been travelling ever since and adding a little fresh cold each day till I have really worked it up into something pretty heavy. Yesterday, I stayed in bed all day and I am taking hot salt baths every night. I have a most comfortable room on this splendid boat. There is a fire in the room, the bathroom is next. There are plenty of servants, plenty of good food, and I am as well off as if I were at home. I have driven the cold from my head down into my bronchial tubes and I hope to drive it out completely tonight. It is so annoying to be laid up when you are travelling and I am naturally a little more anxious on account of the great amount of influenza there is about. Well, enough of this, I'll be alright soon.

I have been on the boats of a great many of the large steamship lines, and there are none finer than these C.P.R.[3] boats. The two Empresses, Russia and Asia (This is the Asia) are simply gorgeous palaces, with every known comfort. This has been one of the smoothest trip I ever had. It's just like a mill pond. If you look on the map, you will see our course from Shanghai to Manila. All day yesterday we were passing Formosa on our right; and today we have been passing Luzon, the northern part of the Pacific Island group on our right. It is beautifully clear weather and

---

[3] *Canadian Pacific Railway, a travel company that also operated steamships*

uncomfortably hot because no breeze is blowing. The water is so blue and the ripple so white. There are many flying fish just as one sees everywhere in tropical waters. As I wrote from Peking, I little expected to be here at this time; but while there I got a cable imploring me to return to Vladivostok about April 20th for a conference. I at first said "no"; but in thinking it over for a day decided that I would remain. No one can say that I have not done <u>everything</u> I could to help out. Since I have more than a month to wait, I decided to visit the Philipines, so here I am on my way. I have but <u>one single regret</u> and that is that I shall not be able to be home when it means so much to you. But I feel you will say that I did right to stay. I expect to find much to interest me in the Islands particularly because I have known so many of the people who have had to do with the establishment of government there. I'll write you all about it as I go from place to place. I expect to have time to see a great part of the islands.

I have been disappointed in a way in both Japan and China. I should not want to live in either country. I was agreeably surprised at the condition of the Chinese. While begging is evident everywhere, there is much less poverty than I expected to see. The Chinese are wonderful people. Much more attractive and loveable than the Japanese. It is a marvel what they do with their country. Most of the land is low and flat and at times covered with water, but there are hilly sections in which hills like Fairhaven Hill would be completely covered with little terraces and I really believe they would grow enough on one hill to feed a thousand people. Their thrift is beyond anything we know. They literally do not waste anything. In this respect, they are the exact opposite of the Russians who, as I have told you, are the most wasteful people on Earth unless it be the Americans. I think they could teach us many, many things about plowing, fertilizing, irrigating, etc.

They are so thorough and everything is in the most orderly shape. Both men and women work in the fields and children, of course. It was Spring plowing season in the North of China when I came through and everybody was busy. <u>There are no fences</u> and they use one horse to plow

– not a single inch is lost. They use their hands and feet a great deal in their garden patches.

There is so much land in Manchuria one wonders why the people do not move up there and settle that splendid country instead of living in such crowded conditions in and about the great cities.

I have visited up-to-date Mukden, Tientsin (Tianjin), Peking, Shanghai and I hope later to visit Hong Kong, Canton and some of the larger cities of the South. Of those I will write you later.

March 19th, 9 a.m.

Here we are docked at Manila – very hot and sultry, bright sunshine. Cold much better. More soon.

Love and kisses to all, Henry Ooooo

Letter from Manila, March 22, 1919

Dear Helen,

I am enclosing three papers

1. Receipt for rubles received from L. Turovsky.
2. Statement of costs of certain articles I got in Russia.
3. Receipt for shipment of these goods.

In regard to the first paper, if anything should happen to me, I want my estate to pay Mrs. Turovsky although I am not legally bound to do so. If I should have any accident, I do not want her to lose the money for it comes from her son and is his savings. I took it for delivery, however, without responsibility. I have not yet sold all the rubles, only the Kerensky for which I got the equivalent in U.S. money of $160. I expect to do better with the other (old) money. I wish, therefore, if anything happens to me, you would see that Mrs. Turovsky gets $500 in the U.S. currency for the 5000 rubles.

The other two papers are to be held until I return or if anything should happen they will give you the necessary information to get the goods out of bond by paying the required duty.

I am also enclosing a clipping about an earthquake which we had here yesterday. I tell you it felt queer to have things under you begin to shake.

I bought my ticket for home on the C.P.R, Empress of Russia sailing from Yokohama approximately May 9th due Vancouver May 19th. Boston about May 24th. I'll cable you when I sail.

I am leaving for Bagino tomorrow morning.

I have seen many things Mrs. Forbes started here: his Manila house, the polo clubhouse and grounds, also a game of polo.

I'll write you more about these things later.

Love to all,

Henry Ooooo

Letter from Hong Kong, China, March 31, 1919

Dear Helen,

I arrived here at 10 this morning having left Manila at 10 a.m. Saturday – just two days. I have travelled a good many miles by sea in the last year, but yesterday was the most uncomfortable day I have spent. It was a big, comfortable boat, but one of the meanest days I have ever seen. The sea was rolling badly and there was a strong North East gale. The boat pitched frightfully and though I went to every meal, I was most uncomfortable.

The harbour of Hong Kong is remarkable. You wind in among a series of little islands – very high and perfectly bare. Then the city itself is crowded like a fringe around the front of very steep mountains and the residences are stuck up on the sides of the mountains, clear up to the top. Some of the streets run up and down the hill and the others around parallel to the seashore – making a great scheme like the stadium although spread out a great deal more like this.

I am going to try to find some photographs that will give you an idea. I am stopping at a quiet little hotel about half way up the mountain, kept by an American woman. Nothing grand, but seems to be clean and quiet. Hotels generally throughout the Orient are crowded. Tomorrow expect to go up to Canton, the largest city of China. I will write you about that after I come back. I wrote you that I had passage on the Empress of Russia, a CPR boat leaving Yokohama about May 19th for Vancouver. Now I have just been informed that the British government have commandeered these boats to carry our troops form Vladivostok to Canada. So I am out again. I hope, however, to get to Vladivostok and make arrangements to get on the same boat. I may get home even earlier in this way than by the other plan – but I don't know and can't find out till I reach Vladivostok.

Thursday, 4th

Just returned from a very pleasant and interesting trip up the river to Canton. It is the largest city in China, and it is simply unbelievable how closely people are packed together.

500,000 are said to live on the "sand pans" (small boats that lie in the river). Poor little tots are born, live and die and never put their feet on the earth. I doubt this very much – yet they doubtless spend most of their lives on these small boats. I think the Chinese are great people – the best I have seen in the Orient. They work so hard, live on so little, save every single speck of everything – absolutely nothing wasted. You know how that appeals to me!

This morning I visited Hong Kong University. Fine buildings, 250 students – all nationalities – good library and laboratories.

Expect to leave here Saturday 11 a.m. for Shanghai. Will write you again from there.

Love to all, 2 months more and I'll be with you. Henry Ooooo

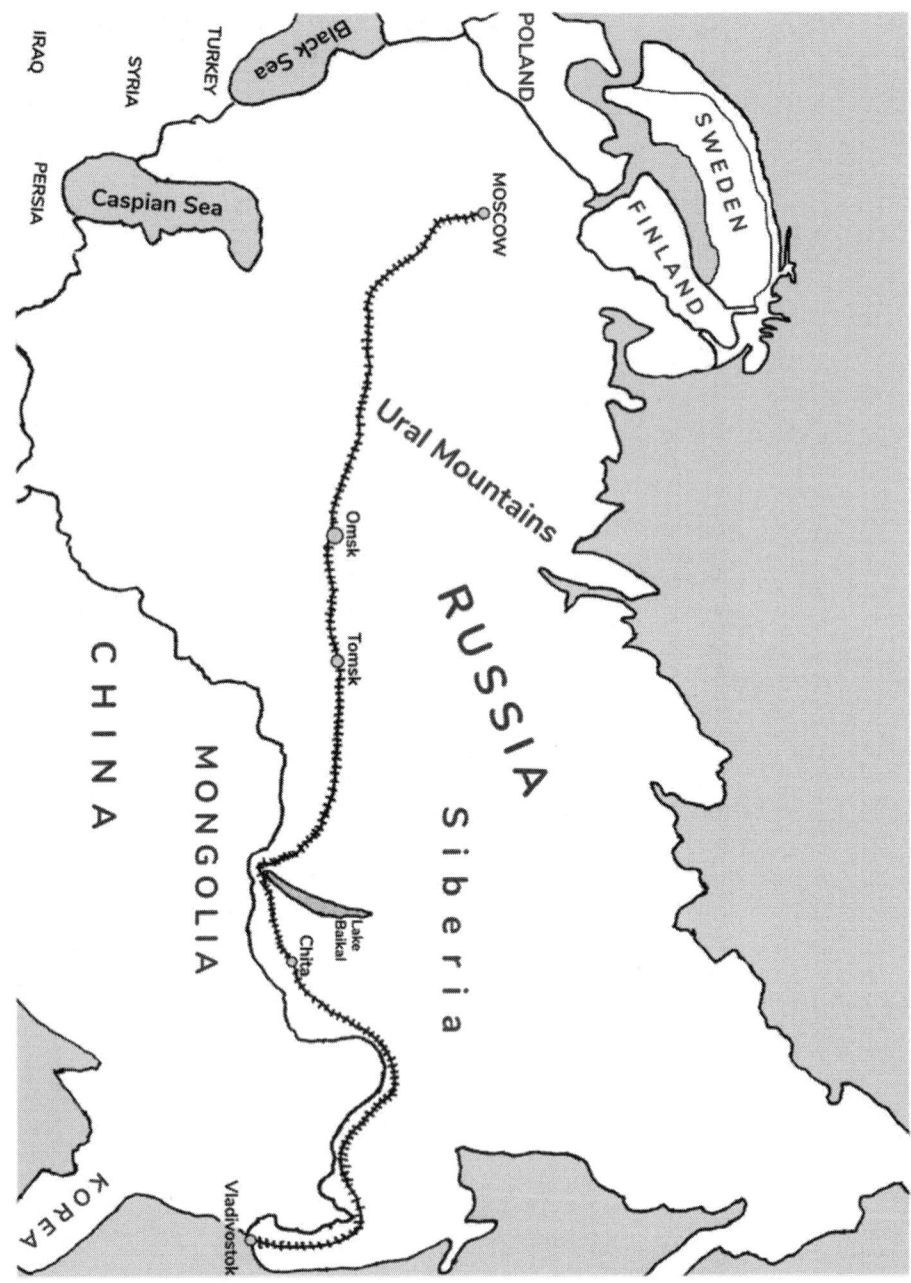

Fig. 20: Sketch map of Russia showing locations mentioned in the letters and path of the Trans-Siberian Railway

Henry Smith Thompson
1873-1944

Henry Smith Thompson, my grandfather, was born in Ohio in 1873. His father was the postmaster of Senecaville. He came from a farming area and maintained an interest in farming all his life. He attended Harvard College, reputedly shovelling coal to pay for his tuition fees. He graduated from Harvard in 1899 and then entered the administrative department of the university. Subsequently, he formed the firm of Eustis and Thompson and became active in the management of electrical properties in the Connecticut Valley. In 1916, he was appointed a member of the Commission on Public Safety of Massachusetts and a representative of the Commission for the Relief of Belgium, headed by Herbert Hoover. In 1918, he joined the American Red Cross service with the assimilated rank of major, and was assigned to refugee relief work in the territory between Lake Baikal and the Ural Mountains in Siberia, remaining there until March 1919. For his war service he was decorated by the Belgian and Russian governments.

Fig. 21: Portrait of Henry S Thompson, 1917

On his return, he turned to land development in Colorado and New Mexico and later was president of a small railroad there. In 1921, he became connected with industrial medicine work under the direction of the Harvard Medical School and was appointed secretary of the school soon afterward. In 1923, he joined a

Fig. 22: Thompson in later life

firm of investment bankers and later became a partner in which he was connected until his death. As a resident of Concord, Massachusetts, he was a member of the water and sewer commission and was active in Red Cross affairs. He was also president of the Harvard Cooperative Society from 1922 until his death. He remained affiliated with many Harvard clubs and institutions as well as being active in local affairs, such as the Massachusetts Agricultural Club.

My grandfather married Helen Sargent Apthorp in 1907 and had four children, the youngest of whom was on the way while he was posted to Siberia. Together they settled in Concord, Massachusetts where they owned a farm and he indulged his fancy for grape growing.

On reading my grandfather's letters, it is quite evident that his experiences in Siberia in 1918-1919 had a profound effect upon him. He had never been involved directly in this kind of philanthropic work. He found it deeply disturbing to see the suffering of refugees and did everything within his power to help them. At times, it appears that he was overwhelmed by the job, but was determined to do his best and complete his work there. In his letters to his young children, whom he calls 'chicks', he suggests that one of the most important things we can do in life is to help others less fortunate than ourselves.

Fig. 23: Thompson as a young businessman

These letters are unique in that they are a personal account of the tragic plight of refugees in Siberia in 1918-1919. Some of the descriptions show how desperate they were and give a vivid picture of their suffering. We can read of similar situations today, but this account seems to illustrate how painful it is to see such suffering and how difficult this work can be.

Some personal notes

I was born and grew up in Concord, Massachusetts. My grandfather was part of the liberal tradition of public service which has survived in New England today.

I have myself found many opportunities to explore the world in a volunteer capacity. As a teenager, I volunteered on a Quaker workcamp and went on an exchange programme to England.

The late sixties were a time of political turmoil and we were all inspired to make the world a better place. At this time, I decided that I would become a teacher.

I have taught in the United States, England and Uganda. Throughout my career, I have felt that it has been possible to influence young people and inspire them to greater achievements. I have also enjoyed and appreciated the chance to learn about other cultures through personal involvement with students and friends from other countries.

In sympathy with my grandfather, I have taken an active part in supporting the cause of refugees. While in Uganda, I saw the disruption that was caused by the expulsion of the Asian population by Amin. Since that time, I have become involved in volunteer work with Freedom from Torture and Asylum Welcome and Oxford Welcomes Refugees.

For these reasons, these letters resonate with my own values and experiences. As my grandfather was touched by the suffering of the refugees who surrounded him, I also feel that it is important to offer help to those whose lives have been so cruelly disrupted.

Hilary Hullah
Oxford, 20th April 2021